T0219968

Microsoft Computer Vision APIs Distilled

Getting Started with Cognitive Services

Alessandro Del Sole

Apress®

Microsoft Computer Vision APIs Distilled

Alessandro Del Sole
Cremona, Italy

ISBN-13 (pbk): 978-1-4842-3341-2   ISBN-13 (electronic): 978-1-4842-3342-9
https://doi.org/10.1007/978-1-4842-3342-9

Library of Congress Control Number: 2017962422

Cover image designed by Freepik

Managing Director: Welmoed Spahr
Editorial Director: Todd Green
Acquisitions Editor: Joan Murray
Development Editor: Laura Berendson
Coordinating Editor: Jill Balzano
Copy Editor: Kim Wimpsett
Compositor: SPi Global
Indexer: SPi Global
Artist: SPi Global

Distributed to the book trade worldwide by Springer Science+Business Media New York, 233 Spring Street, 6th Floor, New York, NY 10013. Phone 1-800-SPRINGER, fax (201) 348-4505, e-mail orders-ny@springer-sbm.com, or visit www.springeronline.com. Apress Media, LLC is a California LLC and the sole member (owner) is Springer Science + Business Media Finance Inc (SSBM Finance Inc). SSBM Finance Inc is a **Delaware** corporation.

For information on translations, please e-mail rights@apress.com, or visit www.apress.com/rights-permissions.

Apress titles may be purchased in bulk for academic, corporate, or promotional use. eBook versions and licenses are also available for most titles. For more information, reference our Print and eBook Bulk Sales web page at www.apress.com/bulk-sales.

Any source code or other supplementary material referenced by the author in this book is available to readers on GitHub via the book's product page, located at www.apress.com/9781484233412. For more detailed information, please visit www.apress.com/source-code.

Printed on acid-free paper

To my wonderful Angelica, who brings sunshine into my life.

Contents

About the Author

Alessandro Del Sole has been a Microsoft Most Valuable Professional (MVP) since 2008, and he is a Xamarin Certified Mobile Developer and Microsoft Certified Professional. Awarded MVP of the Year in 2009, 2010, 2011, 2012, and 2014, he is internationally considered a Visual Studio expert and a .NET authority. He has authored many books on programming with Visual Studio, Xamarin, and .NET, and he blogs and writes technical articles about Microsoft developer topics in Italian and English for many developer sites, including MSDN Magazine and the Visual Basic Developer Center from Microsoft. He is a frequent speaker at Microsoft technical conferences.

Acknowledgments

Writing books is hard work, not only for the author but for all the people involved in the reviews and in the production process.

Therefore, I would like to thank Joan Murray, Jill Balzano, Laura Berendson, and everyone at Apress who contributed to publishing this book and made the process much more pleasant.

A very special thanks to the technical editor, who did an incredible job walking through every single sentence and every single line of code, providing invaluable contributions to this book's contents.

I would also like to thank the Technical Evangelism team of the Italian subsidiary of Microsoft and my Microsoft MVP lead, Cristina G. Herrero, for their continuous support and encouragement for my activities.

As the community leader of the Italian Visual Studio Tips & Tricks community (www.visualstudiotips.net), I want to say "thank you!" to the other team members (Laura La Manna, Renato Marzaro, Antonio Catucci, Igor Damiani) and to our followers for keeping our passion strong for sharing knowledge and for helping people solve problems in their daily work.

Thanks to all my friends, who are always ready to encourage me even if they are not developers.

Finally, special thanks to my girlfriend, Angelica, who knows how strong my passion for technology is and who never complains about the time I spend writing.

Introduction

Artificial intelligence is growing in importance, and many devices and applications already use sophisticated algorithms to improve people's lives and business tasks.

As developers, getting familiar with artificial intelligence is extremely important so we can start thinking about the next generation of applications and about our customers' needs. Among others, Microsoft Cognitive Services offer a wide range of sophisticated algorithms that can be consumed through the standard REST approach. Therefore, they can be used to develop intelligent cross-platform and cross-device apps, such as mobile apps and web applications in any programming language and on any development platform. Specifically, this book covers the Computer Vision API, a service capable of understanding and interpreting the content of any images, providing a natural language description that can even be sent to other Microsoft services, such as the Speech API or the Translation API to make your app speak about the analysis result in a different language. The Computer Vision service can also analyze images for optical character recognition to detect print and handwritten words and sentences, and it includes domain-specific models that help you identify important people or landmarks in a picture and that in the future could be extended according to your needs.

The Computer Vision API, as well as other Microsoft Cognitive Services, relies on the REST standard and returns JSON data. This means these powerful services can be consumed by any application, on any platform, and with any programming languages and frameworks supporting REST and JSON.

This book is for developers working with the Microsoft stack. You will find explanations and examples based on C# and .NET. After an introduction to Cognitive Services in Chapter 1 and to the Computer Vision API in Chapter 2, in Chapter 3 you will learn how to write C# code that sends images to the Computer Vision service for analysis, and the code you'll write can be used across different platforms such as the .NET Framework, .NET Core, and Xamarin. In fact, Chapters 4 and 5 provide examples of how to include artificial intelligence based on the Computer Vision API in your iOS, Android, and Windows 10 mobile apps using Xamarin, and in your web apps using ASP.NET Core.

As you might know, now you can write C# code on Windows, macOS, and Linux (and its more popular distributions) with the .NET Core cross-platform runtime. For this reason, you can choose one of the following system configurations:

- A Windows PC with Visual Studio 2017

- A Mac with Visual Studio for Mac

- An Ubuntu or other Linux system with Visual Studio Code and .NET Core 2.0

- A Windows PC with Visual Studio Code and .NET Core 2.0

- A Mac with Visual Studio Code and .NET Core 2.0

Most of C# examples you find in this book are available to all these systems and configurations, except for the Xamarin example, which you will be able to use only on Windows and macOS.

After reading this book, you will be able to get started with AI services from Microsoft and develop your own powerful, intelligent apps.

■ ■ ■

CHAPTER 1

Introducing Microsoft Cognitive Services

Without a doubt, artificial intelligence (AI) is an important part of information technology today. It certainly will be more and more important in the future, but it's already being used in many ways, so you, as a developer, should learn about what tools and services are available to build next-generation applications.

Most of the world's software giants offer AI solutions, and Microsoft has an interesting range of services and tools that will simplify the way you build and implement solutions based on artificial intelligence. This chapter provides a high-level overview of what Microsoft provides for AI, with a detailed description of the Cognitive Services APIs. This serves as the base for the next chapter, where you will walk through the Computer Vision API.

Introducing the Microsoft AI Platform

Microsoft provides the AI Platform (`www.microsoft.com/en-us/AI/ai-platform`), a set of services and tools that applications can consume across platforms. The AI Platform includes services for creating bots; services for machine learning and deep learning; and services for analyzing pictures, real-time videos, and speeches.

More specifically, the Microsoft AI Platform includes the following:

- The Bot Framework, which allows you to build and connect conversational bots and create natural interactions with users (`http://dev.botframework.com/`).

- Cognitive Services, a set of RESTful services capable of recognizing, understanding, and interpreting the content of pictures, speeches, live videos, written text, and much more, with a natural language description (`http://azure.microsoft.com/en-us/services/cognitive-services/`).

- Azure Machine Learning, a robust cloud platform that helps developers build their own custom AI solutions (`http://azure.microsoft.com/en-us/services/machine-learning-services/`).

© Alessandro Del Sole 2018
A. Del Sole, *Microsoft Computer Vision APIs Distilled*,
https://doi.org/10.1007/978-1-4842-3342-9_1

In the next section, you will get an overview of Cognitive Services; then, in Chapter 2, you will start working with the Computer Vision API, which is the real focus of this book.

Introducing Microsoft Cognitive Services

Microsoft Cognitive Services are RESTful services that allow for natural user interaction on any platform on any device.

The Cognitive Services APIs perfectly embody the conversation-as-a-platform vision that Microsoft strongly believes in, by providing a rich set of APIs that allow for processing human language, sentiments, emotions, physical characteristics, audio, and much more. At a higher level, the Cognitive Services APIs are grouped into the categories in Table 1-1.

Table 1-1. *Categories of Microsoft Cognitive Services*

Service Category	Description
Vision	These APIs provide image-processing algorithms that help identify, caption, moderate, understand, and describe pictures and videos with a natural language description (http://azure.microsoft.com/en-us/services/cognitive-services/directory/vision/).
Knowledge	These APIs help you implement a customer's knowledge by finding events, locations, academic papers, and recommendations tailored to a customer's needs (http://azure.microsoft.com/en-us/services/cognitive-services/directory/know/).
Language	These APIs are capable of processing natural language, evaluating sentiments, and understanding a customer's needs (http://azure.microsoft.com/en-us/services/cognitive-services/directory/lang/).
Speech	These APIs enable audio processing with speaker recognition, voice verification, and audio conversion into text (http://azure.microsoft.com/en-us/services/cognitive-services/directory/speech/).
Search	Based on the Bing search engine services, these APIs allow you to implement image search, news search, video search, and autosuggestions (http://azure.microsoft.com/en-us/services/cognitive-services/directory/search/).

Each category contains a number of specialized sets of APIs. Describing all these sets is out of the scope of this book; therefore, you can read more by visiting the related web pages for each category. It is worth mentioning the available APIs in the Vision category, because this book focuses on the Computer Vision API, included in this category, so that you have an overview of what these APIs can do. Table 1-2 summarizes the specialized APIs available in the Vision category.

Table 1-2. *The Vision APIs*

API	Description
Computer Vision API	Provides image-processing algorithms that help you understand, analyze, and describe images with natural language response. It includes optical character recognition (OCR) and celebrity recognition (`http://azure.microsoft.com/en-us/services/cognitive-services/computer-vision/`).
Content Moderator	Provides automated content moderation for images, videos, and text (`http://azure.microsoft.com/en-us/services/cognitive-services/content-moderator/`).
Video API	Provides powerful APIs that are capable of improving video quality as well as detecting and identifying faces and other elements within videos (`http://azure.microsoft.com/en-us/services/cognitive-services/video-api/`). This is currently a preview service.
Video Indexer	Allows you to maximize video interactions and insights, helping make video content more discoverable (`http://azure.microsoft.com/en-us/services/cognitive-services/video-indexer/`). This is currently a preview service.
Face API	Detects, identifies, analyzes, and organizes faces in an image (`http://azure.microsoft.com/en-us/services/cognitive-services/face/`).
Emotion API	Detects people's emotions in an image, based on face detection (`http://azure.microsoft.com/en-us/services/cognitive-services/emotion/`).
Custom Vision Service	Enables custom image processing based on tags and labels (`http://azure.microsoft.com/en-us/services/cognitive-services/custom-vision-service/`). This service is currently in preview.

The Cognitive Services APIs are offered through the Microsoft Azure cloud platform, including the Computer Vision API discussed in this book. As an implication, you will need an active Azure subscription to work with such services. You can request a free Azure trial at `http://azure.microsoft.com/en-us/free/`. This is also required to complete the code examples in the next chapter, so in Chapter 2 I will explain how to configure your Azure subscription to get your personal access keys.

Introducing Development Tools and Platforms

Based on the REST approach and on the JSON standard data exchange format, Cognitive Services can be potentially consumed by any application, on any device, on any operating system, and through any development platform and programming language that supports both REST and JSON.

As a developer working with the .NET technologies, you can consume such services in any kind of .NET application and with all the .NET languages such as C#, F#, and Visual Basic. Having said that, you have three major options.

- On Windows, you can use Visual Studio 2017 as the development environment for full support to all the .NET project types. If you do not have an MSDN subscription, you can download the Community edition for free (`www.visualstudio.com/downloads/`).

- On macOS, you can use Visual Studio for Mac as a development environment supporting cross-platform development with .NET Core and mobile app development with Xamarin. You can download the Community edition for free (`www.visualstudio.com/vs/visual-studio-mac/`).

- On Linux (and its most popular distributions), macOS, and Windows, you can use Visual Studio Code (`http://code.visualstudio.com`) for C# development over .NET Core.

In this book, I will showcase two sample applications based on Xamarin and .NET Core, so I encourage you to use Visual Studio 2017 on Windows or Visual Studio for Mac on macOS. If you instead work on Linux, no worries: you will be able to follow all the examples related to .NET Core by using Visual Studio Code. In all cases, you will be able to learn how to query the Computer Vision service in C# with a console application in Chapter 3.

Summary

Microsoft has offered many high-quality and powerful AI services and tools over the years, and the AI Platform represents the state of the art for Microsoft. This chapter provided a brief introduction to the AI Platform, describing the tools and services it includes.

An introduction to Cognitive Services was also provided, along with a mention of the services offered in the Vision category so that you can better understand how the Computer Vision API fits into the Microsoft offerings. Finally, you learned what tools and platforms you need to consume Cognitive Services in your applications. In the next chapter, you will learn how the Computer Vision API works, and you will learn how to configure your Azure subscription to get your access keys.

CHAPTER 2

■ ■ ■

Getting Started with the Computer Vision API

Imagine you want to build apps that help people with disabilities to understand what's around them and to read papers on their behalf.

Now imagine you want to build apps that help kids learn about the world from pictures, making sure that adult content is excluded. Then, imagine you want to build apps that help people learn a foreign language by providing natural language sentences that describe an image. Finally, imagine you work on a police force and want to build a custom solution that helps your department identify criminals based on images.

These are only a few examples of how artificial intelligence could help solve a number of problems, but they are enough to make you understand the purpose of the Computer Vision API. Combined with other Cognitive Services APIs, you have infinite opportunities. This chapter first describes how the Computer Vision API works, and then it describes how to configure your Azure subscription and expose a Computer Vision API endpoint that can be consumed by any application.

Understanding the Computer Vision API

As well as with every other cognitive service, the Computer Vision API has its own portal; you can reach it at http://azure.microsoft.com/en-us/services/cognitive-services/computer-vision/. Here you will find shortcuts to the documentation and examples, but I will want focus on the API reference available at http://bit.ly/2sBtryy. When you open this page, you will see a list of available operations that you can execute against images.

Technically speaking, with the Computer Vision API, you invoke a RESTful service by uploading an image or pointing to an existing image URL and sending GET and POST HTTP requests depending on the type of analysis you want to execute against the image.

The Computer Vision service will return a JSON response that contains the analysis results. The service URL varies depending on your closest region, and an active Azure subscription is required to activate the keys you'll use in the HTTP requests. You will configure your Azure subscription in the next section; for now focus on the available types of analysis you can perform on images and their corresponding HTTP requests, described in Table 2-1.

© Alessandro Del Sole 2018
A. Del Sole, *Microsoft Computer Vision APIs Distilled*,
https://doi.org/10.1007/978-1-4842-3342-9_2

Table 2-1. *Available Analysis Types with the Computer Vision API*

Type	Description	HTTP Verb	Endpoint
Analyze Image	Analyzes an image for adult and racial content, face detection, tags, and dominant colors	POST	`https://[location].api.cognitive.microsoft.com/vision/v1.0/analyze[?visualFeatures][&details][&language]`
Describe Image	Generates a description of an image in human-readable language with complete sentences	POST	`https://[location].api.cognitive.microsoft.com/vision/v1.0/describe[?maxCandidates]`
Get Thumbnail	Generates a thumbnail from the specified image	POST	`https://[location].api.cognitive.microsoft.com/vision/v1.0/generateThumbnail[?width][&height][&smartCropping`
List Domain Specific Models	Gets the list of the currently supported domain-specific models, such as the celebrity and landmark recognizers	GET	`https://[location].api.cognitive.microsoft.com/vision/v1.0/models`
OCR	Performs optical character recognition over an image and stores detected text into machine-usable characters	POST	`https://[location].api.cognitive.microsoft.com/vision/v1.0/ocr[?language][&detectOrientation ]`
Recognize Domain Specific Content	Analyzes a picture to retrieve domain-specific content such as celebrities or landmarks	POST	`https://[location].api.cognitive.microsoft.com/vision/v1.0/models/{model}/analyze`
Recognize Handwritten Text	Executes handwritten text recognition	POST	`https://[location].api.cognitive.microsoft.com/vision/v1.0/recognizeText[?handwriting]`
Tag Image	Generates a list of words that are relevant to the content of the specified image	POST	`https://[location].api.cognitive.microsoft.com/vision/v1.0/tag`

Each of the operations listed in 2-1 is invoked as a specific endpoint. Every time you want to invoke the Computer Vision service, you will need to replace the [location]. api.cognitive.microsoft.com literal in the URL with one of the following, depending on the nearest Azure region:

- westus.api.cognitive.microsoft.com for the West US region

- westus2.api.cognitive.microsoft.com for the West US 2 region

- eastus.api.cognitive.microsoft.com for the East US region

- eastus2.api.cognitive.microsoft.com for the East US 2 region

- westcentralus.api.cognitive.microsoft.com for the West Central US region

- southcentralus.api.cognitive.microsoft.com for the South Central US region

- westeurope.api.cognitive.microsoft.com for the West Europe region

- northeurope.api.cognitive.microsoft.com for the North Europe region

- southeastasia.api.cognitive.microsoft.com for the South East Asia region

- eastasia.api.cognitive.microsoft.com for the East Asia region

- australiaeast.api.cognitive.microsoft.com for the East Australia region

- brazilsouth.api.cognitive.microsoft.com for the Brazil South region

The list of available URLs might vary in the future if the number of regions is increased or reorganized. You can look at the full list of Azure regions (http://azure. microsoft.com/en-us/regions/), but keep in mind that not all Microsoft products are available in all regions, and this is the case with Cognitive Services too.

Performing HTTP Requests

As a general rule, to analyze an image with one of the operations listed in 2-1, you send an HTTP request to the related endpoint. For example, suppose you want to generate a list of tags relevant to the content of an image. You would use the following endpoint (replacing [location] with the Azure region's domain name):

https://[location].api.cognitive.microsoft.com/vision/v1.0/tag

Each request will contain the following headers:

- Content-Type, an optional string that describes the media type of the body sent to the API, such as application/JSON or application/octet-stream

- Ocp-Apim-Subscription-Key, a mandatory string that contains a valid subscription key that provides access to the API and that you will get through the Azure portal

The request body is normally passed with a POST request and can be either a raw image binary or an image URL supplied via JSON syntax. For example, if you want to pass the URL of an existing image, the body of your request will be as follows:

```
{"url":"http://onewebsite.com/image1.jpg"}
```

The MIME type for this body is application/JSON. In real-world development, you will use classes that allow for data exchange through the network, such as HttpClient in C# and Java, or web debugging applications such as Postman to send your requests, so you will not need to worry how to manually create headers and request bodies. For example, you can send a request with Postman and expect a JSON response, as demonstrated in Figure 2-1, where you can also see where and how to supply the content type and the subscription key (the latter is partially obfuscated for privacy reasons).

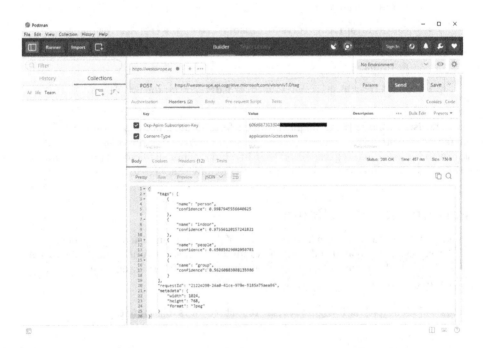

Figure 2-1. *Sending an HTTP request to the Computer Vision API with Postman*

In this particular case, you will get a JSON response that contains an array of tags, each with a name and confidence percentage. You also get additional information, such as the request's unique identifier and the image size. Other operations provided by the Computer Vision API can be invoked in a similar way, changing the endpoint and providing the required parameters.

Whether you work with a debugging tool like Postman or with specialized classes in your favorite programming language, you will need to supply the information described earlier. In the next chapter, you will see how to perform all the available operations from C# with the HttpClient class and how to parse the JSON response in code. In the meantime, you can try the API testing console included in the Computer Vision API portal (available at http://bit.ly/2sBtryy). To accomplish this, select an operation on the left and then click the button that represents your Azure region near the "Open API testing console" box. At this point, a series of text boxes will appear, and you will find guidance of how to fill them out and create a POST request to the service. You will then be able to see the JSON response if the operation succeeds, or you will see an error message if it fails.

Handling the HTTP Response

Like any other RESTful service, Computer Vision returns an HTTP code and a description that allows you to understand whether an operation succeeded or not, and the reason. Table 2-2 summarizes the most common HTTP status codes that you might get back when working with Computer Vision.

Table 2-2. *Computer Vision Status Codes*

HTTP Status Code	Description
200 (Success)	The requested operation completed successfully, and an analysis result was returned as JSON.
400 (Bad Request)	The requested operation failed with one of the following self-explanatory errors: InvalidImageUrl, InvalidImageFormat, InvalidImageSize, NotSupportedImage.
415 (Unsupported Media Type)	The requested operation failed because the supplied Content-Type header does not match the image content.
500 (Internal Server Error)	The requested operation failed with one of the following self-explanatory errors: FailedToProcess, Timeout, InternalServerError.
401 (Unauthorized)	The requested operation could not be executed because an invalid subscription key was supplied.

It is important to mention that you could get an error 400 (Bad Request) if the image you supply does not satisfy these minimum requirements:

- The image must be PNG, JPG, BMP, or GIF.

- The image must be greater than 50 × 50.

- The file size must be less than 4Mb.

So, as a best practice, make sure your applications check whether an image satisfies the minimum requirements before requesting a Computer Vision analysis operation.

Configuring Your Azure Subscription

Before you can try the Computer Vision API, you need to activate a subscription key in the Microsoft Azure management portal. Assuming you already have an active Azure subscription, you can log into the portal at `http://portal.azure.com`.

Once you have logged in, click New, then click AI + Cognitive Services (see Figure 2-2), and finally click Computer Vision API.

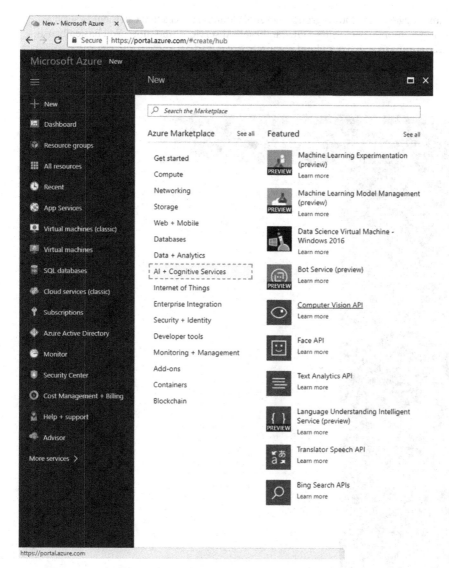

Figure 2-2. *Creating a new Computer Vision API subscription*

At this point, you will need to specify a name for the new Computer Vision API service, the location, the pricing tier, and a resource group. You can enter a name of your choice, or **MyVisionService** like in the current example, as demonstrated in Figure 2-3. Notice that, as the location, you will need to select the nearest Azure region to you. For the pricing tier, I suggest you to use the F0 plan, which is not charged (click "View full pricing details" to get more information). For the resource group, you will be allowed to create a new one or select an existing group. In the current example, I'm creating a new resource group for convenience. If you are new to Azure, it is worth mentioning that, as

11

the name suggests, a resource group is a set of cloud resources that can include services, applications, mobile back ends, SQL databases, AI services, and more. You basically use resource groups to keep your cloud resources organized.

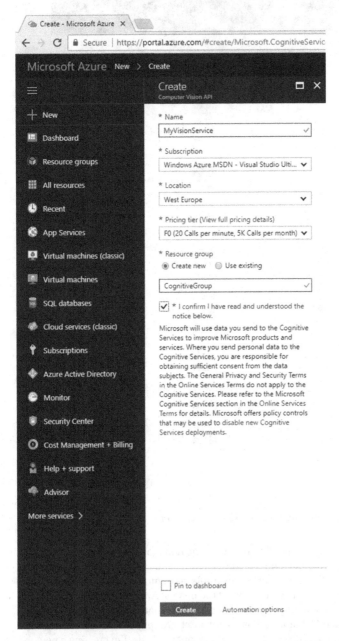

Figure 2-3. *Supplying information for the new Computer Vision API*

When you click Create, the service will be provisioned. In Figure 2-4 you can see a shortcut called "Show access keys" that you will want to click to generate your subscription keys, which are required to access the Computer Vision API.

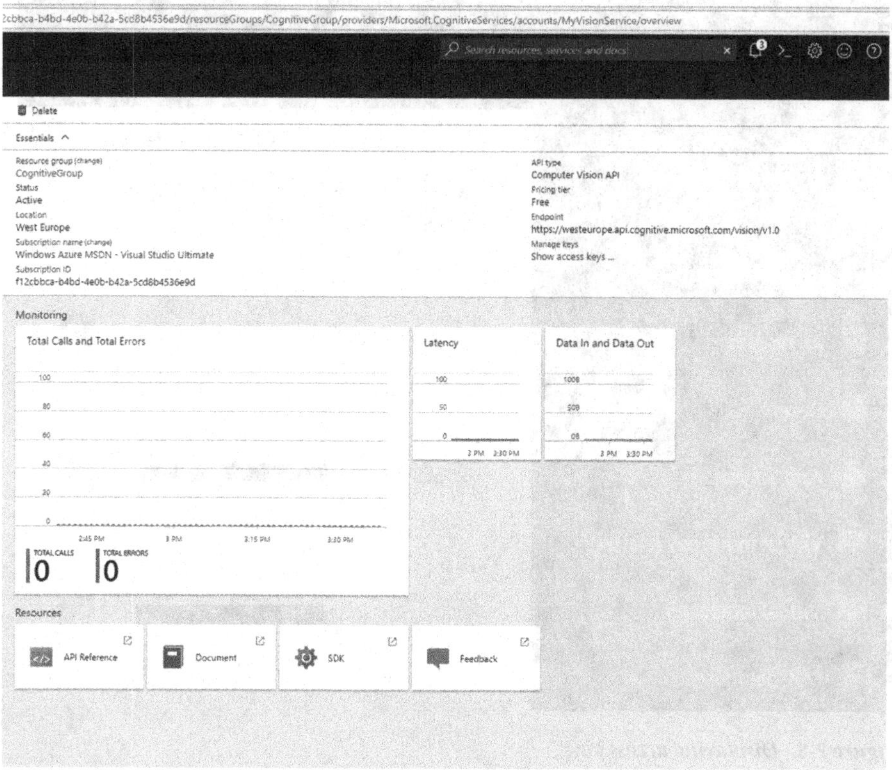

Figure 2-4. The service details and the "Show access keys" shortcut

When you click "Show access keys," you will see two autogenerated keys. You will be able to use them in your HTTP requests interchangeably, and you can regenerate these keys with the Regenerate Key1 and Regenerate Key2 buttons in the toolbar (see Figure 2-5).

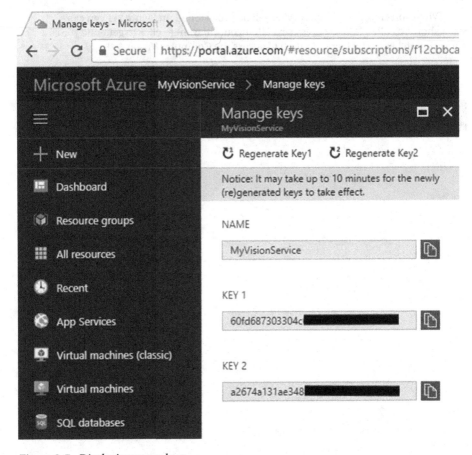

Figure 2-5. *Displaying access keys*

You can copy these keys to the clipboard for later reuse. Obviously, these include sensitive information, so you should always keep them safe. You do not need any other configuration to use the Computer Vision API, because you will simply invoke the service URL, passing the subscription key.

Summary

The Computer Vision API allows you to execute a number of analysis operations on images. To accomplish this, you invoke an endpoint whose URL varies depending on the Azure region you want to work with. Generally speaking, you create an HTTP request where the header contains the subscription key and the content type, whereas the body contains the image you want to analyze, either as a URL or as binary data.

Regardless of the operation you requested, you will receive a JSON response that contains the analysis result (and that you will need to parse) if the operation succeeds. If it fails, the service returns the appropriate HTTP status code with a description. The subscription key you need to invoke the Computer Vision API can be generated in the Azure management portal, where you get two keys that you can copy to the clipboard or regenerate at any time. In the next chapter, you will start performing real HTTP requests against the Computer Vision API service in C#, executing all the available analysis operations and learning how to parse and interpret the JSON result.

■ ■ ■

CHAPTER 3

Invoking the Computer Vision API from C#

Being RESTful services, all the Cognitive Services APIs, including the Computer Vision API, can be queried by any programming language that supports HTTP requests and the JSON format. This chapter is all about C# and explains how to analyze an image with C# code that can be used across platforms. You will learn how to execute all the analysis operations that Computer Vision provides, using all the major IDEs from Microsoft.

The first step is setting up your toolbox, and then you will be able to write some code.

■ **Note**   Always be careful of how you use Cognitive Services and of the images you upload. Microsoft has strict terms that you must read before working with the API, available at http://azure.microsoft.com/en-us/support/legal/cognitive-services-terms.

Getting Sample Images

You are obviously totally free to use your own images for analysis, and I do encourage you to do so, but in case you do not have any useful image files, I have prepared three for you that are available on my blog.

- *A picture of a seaside landscape*: http://community.visual-basic.it/images/community_visual-basic_it/Alessandro/184/o_SeasideLandscape.jpg

- *A picture of myself, which will be used to demonstrate face detection*: http://community.visual-basic.it/images/community_visual-basic_it/Alessandro/184/o_AleDelSole.png

- *A picture with some printed text, which will be used to demonstrate optical character recognition*: http://community.visual-basic.it/images/community_visual-basic_it/Alessandro/184/o_OcrSample.jpg

Remember to take a look at the Cognitive Services terms of use before you move any application to production.

Creating a C# Console Application

Because the purpose of this chapter is explaining how to code against the Computer Vision service in C#, it's a good idea to use a console application, which is a platform-independent project type. In the next two chapters, you will see how to create a mobile app and a web app, respectively.

I will now explain how to create a console application with Visual Studio 2017, Visual Studio for Mac, and Visual Studio Code.

■ **Note**   There are many ways in C# to parse JSON markup into .NET objects, with built-in types and with third-party libraries. In this book, I will use the popular Newtonsoft.Json library (`https://www.newtonsoft.com/json`), which is the *de facto* standard to work with JSON in a convenient way.

Creating a Console Application in Visual Studio 2017

Visual Studio 2017 allows you to work with both the .NET Framework and the .NET Core runtimes. I will create a console application based on the .NET Framework, but keep in mind that the same steps apply to .NET Core if you have it installed. Remember that Cognitive Services can be consumed on any platform, which means that applications based on the .NET Framework (such as Windows Presentation Foundation, Windows Forms, and ASP.NET) also can leverage Cognitive Services.

In Visual Studio 2017, select File ➤ New ➤ Project. In the New Project dialog, select the Console App template located under Windows Classic Desktop (see Figure 3-1).

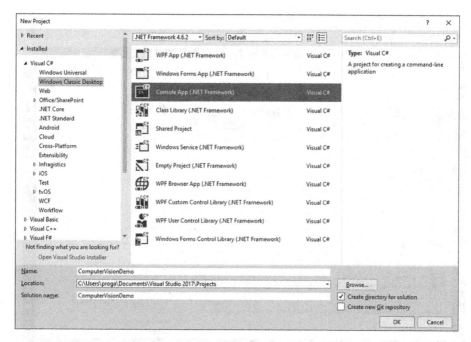

Figure 3-1. *The Console App template in Visual Studio 2017*

Name the new project **ComputerVisionDemo** and then click OK. The Computer Vision API returns the analysis results in JSON format; therefore, you need a way to parse the JSON response and use the result in the form of C# objects. To accomplish this, you can use the popular Newtonsoft.Json library that you can install from NuGet. Right-click the project name in Solution Explorer and then select Manage NuGet Packages. In the NuGet user interface, you should already see the library in the list of packages (if you don't see it, just type its name in the search box). Select the library and then click the Install button on the right, as shown in Figure 3-2.

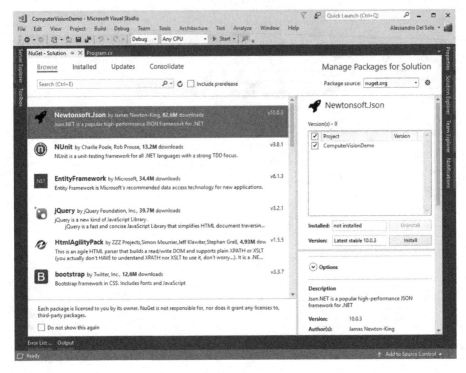

Figure 3-2. *Installing the Newtonsoft.Json NuGet package*

When the package has been installed, add the following using directives in your Program.cs file:

```
using System.Net;
using System.Net.Http;
using Newtonsoft.Json;
using Newtonsoft.Json.Linq;
```

These directives are useful to shorten the invocation to objects you need to call the RESTful service and to work with JSON markup. Everything is now set up in Visual Studio 2017, so let's move to the Visual Studio for Mac environment.

Creating a Console Application in Visual Studio for Mac

Visual Studio for Mac allows you to build .NET Core applications and provides a console application template. To create and configure a console application on macOS, follow these steps:

1. Click File ➤ New Solution.

2. In the New Project dialog, select the App item under .NET Core and then select the Console Application project template, ensuring C# is the selected language (see Figure 3-3).

3. Click Next and, if requested, specify the .NET Core version of your choice. I suggest you use the most recent version available.

4. Enter a project name (see Figure 3-4), such as **ComputerVisionDemo**; finally, click Create.

5. When the project is ready, in the Solution pad right-click the project name and then select Add ➤ NuGet Packages. In the Add Packages dialog (see Figure 3-5), search for the Json.NET package and then click Add Package. Notice that this is the same library discussed previously with Visual Studio 2017, but here it appears with an alternate display name.

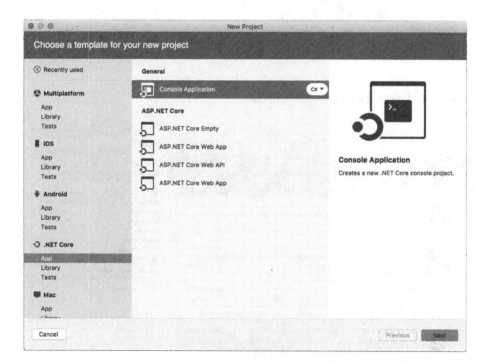

Figure 3-3. *Creating a console app in Visual Studio for Mac*

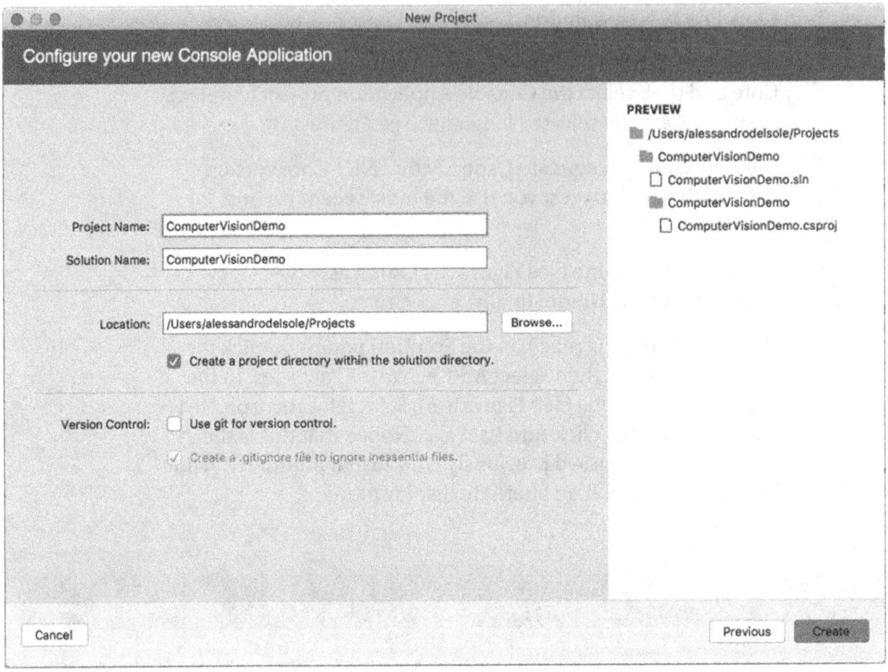

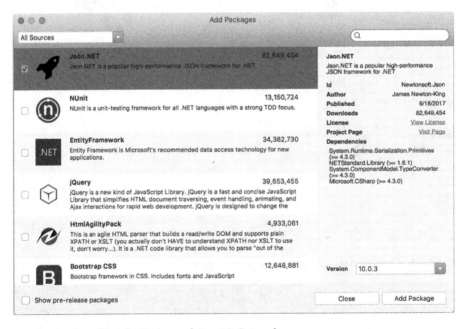

Figure 3-4. *Assigning a name to the new project*

Figure 3-5. *Installing the Newtonsoft.Json NuGet package*

At the top of your `Program.cs` file, add the following using directives, whose purpose is to simplify the access to .NET objects you will be using to call the RESTful service and to work with JSON markup:

```
using System.Net;
using System.Net.Http;
using Newtonsoft.Json;
using Newtonsoft.Json.Linq;
```

Creating a Console Application in Visual Studio Code

Visual Studio Code is a popular, cross-platform tool that allows developers to code in many languages on multiple systems, including Windows, macOS, and Linux (and its most popular distributions). Especially for Linux-based systems, Visual Studio Code is the perfect choice to write C# code based on the .NET Core runtime. I will now demonstrate how to set up a console application on an Ubuntu machine, but the same steps apply to Windows and macOS if you decide to use Visual Studio Code on those systems.

Ubuntu is probably the most popular desktop client distribution of Linux; therefore, it is a good choice for demonstration purposes. If it's not already installed, you will need to download and install both Visual Studio Code (`http://code.visualstudio.com`) and the .NET Core SDK (`www.microsoft.com/net/download/core`).

■ **Note**   If you work on Windows or macOS and want to try Visual Studio Code on Ubuntu, you can create a virtual machine with this OS. You can download the ISO image for Ubuntu from Ubuntu.com.

Assuming you already installed Visual Studio Code and .NET Core 2.0 on your Ubuntu machine, to create a C# console application, follow these steps:

1. With the help of the Files program, locate your personal folder (usually /Home/YourName).

2. Right-click in the folder and then select Open in Terminal. This will open a Terminal window to the folder.

3. Create a new directory that will contain the new project with the following command:

   ```
   > mkdir ComputerVisionDemo
   ```

4. Set the newly created directory as the current directory with the following command:

   ```
   > cd ComputerVisionDemo
   ```

5. Scaffold a new C# console project with the following command:

```
> dotnet new console
```

6. Open Visual Studio Code with the following command:

```
> code.
```

When Visual Studio Code starts, it will open the C# project created previously (see Figure 3-6).

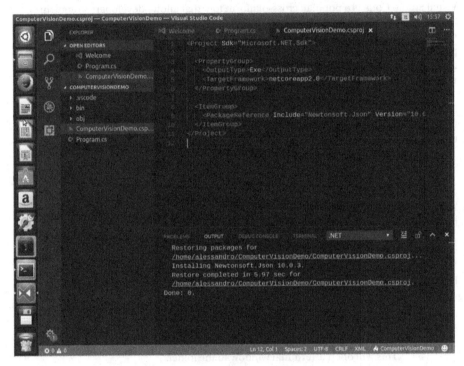

Figure 3-6. The new project opened in Visual Studio Code

Visual Studio Code has no built-in NuGet package manager, so you need to manually edit the project file (.csproj) to add a reference to the Newtonsoft.Json package, which is required to parse the JSON service returned by the Computer Vision API into C# objects. To accomplish this, in the Explorer bar, click the ComputerVisionDemo.csproj file and add the following XML markup to the file:

```
<ItemGroup>
  <PackageReference Include="Newtonsoft.Json" Version="10.0.3" />
</ItemGroup>
```

If you now select File ➤ Save All, Visual Studio Code will ask your permission to restore the missing dependencies so that the Newtonsoft.Json package is installed. Once you have done this, open the Program.cs file and add the following using directives:

```
using System.Net;
using System.Net.Http;
using Newtonsoft.Json;
using Newtonsoft.Json.Linq;
```

They are useful to shorten the invocation to objects you use to call the RESTful service and to work with JSON markup.

Describing and Analyzing Images

The Computer Vision API allows you to describe and analyze images. The difference is simple: describing an image means retrieving a natural language description of the image content, plus a list of relevant tags and details about the image file, such as size and format; analyzing an image includes describing an image, but it also allows for retrieving further details, such as adult and racy content and dominant colors. Let's start with describing an image.

Describing Images

The endpoint you use to describe an image is https://[location].api.cognitive. microsoft.com/vision/v1.0/describe[?maxCandidates], where [location] must be replaced with the domain name of your closest Azure region (see Chapter 2), and maxCandidates represents a query string parameter that establishes how many descriptions should be returned. If this parameter is not specified, the default is 1. Now suppose you want to use the Computer Vision API to describe the landscape picture I provided. This could be done with the following code (see comments):

```
async static Task DescribeImageAsync()
{
    var client = new HttpClient();

    // Return two natural language sentences
    string requestParameters = "maxCandidates=2";

    // Add the subscription key to the header
    client.DefaultRequestHeaders.Add("Ocp-Apim-Subscription-Key",
            "YOUR-KEY-GOES-HERE");

    // Define the API endpoint including the query string parameters
    string uri = "https://westus.api.cognitive.microsoft.com/vision/v1.0/
    describe?" +
                requestParameters;
```

```csharp
HttpResponseMessage response;

// Construct a well-formed JSON key/value pair that
// represents the image URL
JObject imageUrl = new JObject(
                    new JProperty("url",
                    "http://community.visual-basic.it/images/community_
                    visual-basic_it/Alessandro/184/o_SeasideLandscape.
                    jpg"));

// You pass the JSON object above as the request body
using (var content =
    new StringContent(imageUrl.ToString(), Encoding.UTF8, "application/
    json"))
{
    // Add headers
    content.Headers.ContentType = new MediaTypeHeaderValue("application/
    json");

    // Call the endpoint
    response = await client.PostAsync(uri, content);

    // If successful...
    if (response.StatusCode == HttpStatusCode.OK)
    {
        // Read the resulting HTTP content as a string
        string jsonResponse = await response.Content.
        ReadAsStringAsync();

        // Generate fully indented JSON markup from the original
        response
        var parsedJson = JObject.Parse(jsonResponse);

        Console.WriteLine(parsedJson.ToString());
    }

}

Console.ReadLine();
}
```

Common to all requests, you will use the HttpClient class, supplying the appropriate headers, and then you invoke its PostAsync method, passing the endpoint URL and the request body. Notice how the request body is constructed via the JObject class, which allows you to generate well-formed JSON objects. The JProperty class allows you to specify a key/value pair, in this case a key/value pair that represents the image URL. In this case, the code is also supplying the maxCandidates parameter to retrieve multiple descriptions. PostAsync sends an HTTP POST request to the Computer Vision

API; and, if the operation completes successfully, the ReadAsStringAsync method from the Content object (of type HttpContent) returns a JSON string that contains all the details the service was able to return. For the sake of clarity, an invocation to JObject. Parse is done to get a fully indented JSON string, which will appear in the Console window. The previous method must be invoked from the Main method of the Program class as follows:

```
static void Main(string[] args)
{
    DescribeImageAsync().Wait();
}
```

Because you cannot use async and await in the Main method, unless you work with C# 7.1, the call is actually done synchronously using the Wait method.

■ **Note**   C# 7.1 introduces the option to use async and await within the Main method and requires Visual Studio 2017 version 15.3 and higher. I do not use this language version in this book so that you will be able to run the sample code without any issues.

For example, the response I got from this RESTful call is as follows:

```
{
  "description": {
    "tags": [
      "outdoor",
      "boat",
      "scene",
      "water",
      "harbor",
      "filled",
      "ship",
      "dock",
      "carrying",
      "large",
      "small",
      "people",
      "man",
      "docked",
      "many",
      "bunch",
      "group",
      "air",
      "truck",
      "ocean",
      "white",
```

```
    "airplane",
    "plane",
    "body",
    "parked",
    "standing",
    "ramp",
    "board"
  ],
  "captions": [
    {
      "text": "a group of people on a boat in a harbor",
      "confidence": 0.74378581874407157
    },
    {
      "text": "a boat is docked next to a body of water",
      "confidence": 0.74278581874407157
    }
  ]
},
"requestId": "aed5709e-c6c6-43c7-b583-94a2fe0930ad",
"metadata": {
  "width": 3840,
  "height": 2160,
  "format": "Jpeg"
}
}
```

The first JSON element, called description, exposes a tags array that contains a list of tags that the service was able to generate based on the picture content. The second array within description, called captions, contains a list of natural language sentences generated by the service and a confidence level. The higher the level, the higher the confidence of accuracy about the generated sentence. The requestId element is a GUID that uniquely identifies the request, whereas the metadata element contains the image size and format, with self-explanatory properties. In C#, you have many options to access and iterate arrays. However, you can also leverage indexers on the JObject instance to retrieve specific information. For example, the following line retrieves the natural language sentence for the second caption in the array:

```
//Return "a boat is docked next to a body of water"
string description = parsedJson["description"]["captions"][1]["text"].
ToString();
```

As an additional example, you can iterate the list of tags as follows:

```
foreach(var item in parsedJson["description"]["tags"])
{
    Console.WriteLine(item.ToString());
}
```

As you can see, it is outstanding how the Computer Vision API was able to describe the content of an image with natural language sentences and how it returned tags and metadata.

Analyzing Images

Analyzing an image basically works like describing an image, but the difference is that you can retrieve many more details, and therefore you can create more complex query strings. The endpoint for analyzing an image is https://[location].api.cognitive. microsoft.com/vision/v1.0/analyze[?visualFeatures][&details][&language], where [location] must be replaced with the domain name of the closest Azure region. You can also supply a number of optional query string parameters:

- visualFeatures allows you to specify what visual features should be returned. The list of supported features is provided shortly.

- details allows you to include domain-specific details such as celebrity and landmark names. Supported values are Celebrities and Landmarks.

- language provides an option to specify what language the service should use to describe the image. At this writing, supported languages are en (English) and zh (simplified Chinese). If no language is specified, English is the default.

The following is a list of visual features you can specify for deeper image analysis:

- Categories: The service will generate a list of possible categories for the image.

- Tags: The service will generate a list of words related to the image content.

- Faces: The service will retrieve any faces in the image and, if any, will generate coordinates, age, and gender.

- ImageType: The service detects whether an image is clip art or a line drawing.

- Color: The service detects the accent color, dominant color, and whether the image is black and white.

- Adult: The service detects whether the image contains explicit sexual content.

You can combine multiple visual features by separating them with a comma. For example, the following code demonstrates how to retrieve visual features on an image that contains a face:

```
async static Task AnalyzeImageAsync()
{
    var client = new HttpClient();
```

```csharp
// Request parameters. Visual features are comma-separated
string requestParameters = "visualFeatures=Categories,Description,
Color,Faces,Adult";

// Request headers
client.DefaultRequestHeaders.Add("Ocp-Apim-Subscription-Key",
                                    "YOUR-KEY-GOES-HERE");

string uri =
    "https://westus.api.cognitive.microsoft.com/vision/v1.0/analyze?"
    + requestParameters;

HttpResponseMessage response;

JObject imageUrl = new JObject(
                new JProperty("url",
                "http://community.visual-basic.it/images/community_
                visual-basic_it/Alessandro/184/o_AleDelSole.png"));

// Request body
using (var content =
    new StringContent(imageUrl.ToString(), Encoding.UTF8, "application/
    json"))
{
    content.Headers.ContentType = new MediaTypeHeaderValue("application/
    json");
    response = await client.PostAsync(uri, content);

    if(response.StatusCode == HttpStatusCode.OK)
    {
        string jsonResponse = await response.Content.
        ReadAsStringAsync();

        var parsedJson = JObject.Parse(jsonResponse);
        Console.WriteLine(parsedJson.ToString());
    }

}

Console.ReadLine();
}
```

The previous code, used to analyze the picture of me I provided, will return the following JSON:

```json
{
  "categories": [
    {
      "name": "people_portrait",
      "score": 0.91015625
    }
  ],
  "adult": {
    "isAdultContent": false,
    "isRacyContent": false,
    "adultScore": 0.0095219314098358154,
    "racyScore": 0.0099660586565732956
  },
  "description": {
    "tags": [
      "person",
      "man",
      "outdoor",
      "building",
      "camera",
      "smiling",
      "standing",
      "holding",
      "car",
      "street",
      "bus",
      "sitting",
      "wearing",
      "city",
      "black",
      "glasses",
      "large",
      "woman",
      "dog",
      "phone",
      "white"
    ],
    "captions": [
      {
        "text": "a man smiling for the camera",
        "confidence": 0.96098232754013913
      }
    ]
  },
  "requestId": "591dac9c-4729-4964-96f4-726c2c292210",
```

```json
"metadata": {
  "width": 234,
  "height": 234,
  "format": "Png"
},
"faces": [
  {
    "age": 37,
    "gender": "Male",
    "faceRectangle": {
      "left": 53,
      "top": 68,
      "width": 134,
      "height": 134
    }
  }
],
"color": {
  "dominantColorForeground": "White",
  "dominantColorBackground": "Black",
  "dominantColors": [
    "White",
    "Grey"
  ],
  "accentColor": "8D6B3E",
  "isBWImg": false
}
}
```

The JSON markup is pretty simple to understand. In addition to what you already got by describing an image, here you get physical details about the detected faces, gender, age, and coordinates for the face position. Also notice the result for the adult element, where you correctly see that the image does not contain adult or racy content. Just to give you more precise idea, I'm 40 years old as I write this, but the picture was taken when I was 35. The service detected a 37-year-old man, which is a good level of approximation. You can use the same techniques described previously to parse JSON elements and children into JObject instances to make it easier to access JSON arrays and their property/value pairs.

Generating Thumbnails

The Computer Vision API makes it easy to generate image thumbnails. The endpoint is https://[location].api.cognitive.microsoft.com/vision/v1.0/ generateThumbnail[?width][&height][&smartCropping], where [location] is the domain name of your closest Azure region. The width, height, and smartCropping query string parameters represent the thumbnail's width and height and a boolean flag for enabling smart cropping.

As you might expect, in this case the Computer Vision service does not return a plain-text JSON response. The object returned is actually binary data that C# allows you to wrap into a MemoryStream, which you can then elaborate according to your needs, such as displaying the stream content as an image directly or creating a file from the stream using a FileStream. The following code demonstrates how to generate a thumbnail:

```
async static Task GenerateThumbnailAsync()
{
    var client = new HttpClient();

    // Return two natural language sentences
    string requestParameters = "width=320&height=240";

    // Add the subscription key to the header
    client.DefaultRequestHeaders.Add("Ocp-Apim-Subscription-Key",
                                     "YOUR-KEY-GOES-HERE");

    // Define the API endpoint
    string uri = "https://westus.api.cognitive.microsoft.com/vision/v1.0/
    GenerateThumbnail?" +
            requestParameters;

    HttpResponseMessage response;

    // Construct a well-formed JSON key/value pair that
    // represents the image URL
    JObject imageUrl = new JObject(
                    new JProperty("url",
                    "http://community.visual-basic.it/images/community_
                    visual-basic_it/Alessandro/184/o_SeasideLandscape.
                    jpg"));

    // You pass the JSON object above as the request body
    using (var content =
        new StringContent(imageUrl.ToString(), Encoding.UTF8, "application/
        json"))
    {
        // Add headers
        content.Headers.ContentType = new MediaTypeHeaderValue("application/
        json");

        // Call the endpoint
        response = await client.PostAsync(uri, content);
```

```
    // If successful,
    if (response.StatusCode == HttpStatusCode.OK)
    {
        // Get the thumbnail as a MemoryStream
        var binaryResponse = await response.Content.ReadAsStreamAsync();
    }

}

Console.ReadLine();
}
```

Notice how this time you invoke ReadAsStreamAsync to parse the response into a stream object that C# can use.

Tagging Images

The Computer Vision API also allows you to quickly generate tags for an image based on its content, without performing more detailed analysis. The endpoint for tagging is available at https://[location].api.cognitive.microsoft.com/vision/v1.0/tag, and no query string parameters are available. You can write the following code:

```
async static Task TagImageAsync()
{
    var client = new HttpClient();

    // Add the subscription key to the header
    client.DefaultRequestHeaders.Add("Ocp-Apim-Subscription-Key",
            "YOUR-KEY-GOES-HERE");

    // Define the API endpoint
    string uri = "https://westus.api.cognitive.microsoft.com/vision/v1.0/
    tag";

    HttpResponseMessage response;

    // Construct a well-formed JSON key/value pair that
    // represents the image URL
    JObject imageUrl = new JObject(
                    new JProperty("url",
                    "http://community.visual-basic.it/images/community_
                    visual-basic_it/Alessandro/184/o_SeasideLandscape.
                    jpg"));

    // You pass the JSON object above as the request body
    using (var content =
```

```csharp
    new StringContent(imageUrl.ToString(), Encoding.UTF8, "application/
    json"))
{
    // Add headers
    content.Headers.ContentType = new MediaTypeHeaderValue("application/
    json");

    // Call the endpoint
    response = await client.PostAsync(uri, content);

    // If successful,
    if (response.StatusCode == HttpStatusCode.OK)
    {
        // Read the resulting HTTP content as a string
        string jsonResponse = await response.Content.
        ReadAsStringAsync();

        // Generate fully indented JSON markup from the original
        response
        var parsedJson = JObject.Parse(jsonResponse);
        Console.WriteLine(parsedJson.ToString());
    }

}

Console.ReadLine();
}
```

The result you will get is similar to the following JSON:

```json
{
  "tags": [
    {
      "name": "sky",
      "confidence": 0.99912935495376587
    },
    {
      "name": "outdoor",
      "confidence": 0.97800672054290771
    },
    {
      "name": "boat",
      "confidence": 0.94631272554397583
    },
    {
      "name": "scene",
      "confidence": 0.89682495594024658
    },
```

```
  {
    "name": "harbor",
    "confidence": 0.77457839250564575
  }
],
"requestId": "37a85e3b-3008-4166-ba36-7da2c2a78cd7",
"metadata": {
  "width": 3840,
  "height": 2160,
  "format": "Jpeg"
}
}
```

As you can see, this simplified JSON response contains a tags array, where each element contains the word and the confidence level. You can still use the JObject class and the techniques described earlier to access single elements in the array.

Working with Optical Character Recognition

The Computer Vision API provides optical character recognition (OCR). OCR is powerful: Computer Vision can detect text, and it can detect the language, the position of the words, the text orientation, and the angle, in degrees, of the detected text with respect to the closest horizontal or vertical direction. You can leverage OCR by passing the desired image, either as a binary stream or via a URL, to the following endpoint: https://[location].api.cognitive.microsoft.com/vision/v1.0/ocr[?language] [&detectOrientation].

Like with other endpoints, you will replace [location] with the domain name of the closest Azure region, and you can pass the language and detectOrientation query string parameters. The first parameter allows you to specify the language for the text you want to analyze, whereas the second parameter specifies that you also want to retrieve the text orientation. Notice that providing the language is totally optional, as the Computer Vision algorithms will automatically detect the language. It is worth mentioning that this service is powerful enough to retrieve text within other elements in images. In C#, the way you invoke the service is similar to the previous examples.

```
async static Task RecognizeTextAsync()
{
    var client = new HttpClient();

    // Add the subscription key to the header
    client.DefaultRequestHeaders.Add("Ocp-Apim-Subscription-Key",
                                     "YOUR-KEY-GOES-HERE");

    // Define the API endpoint
    string uri = "https://westus.api.cognitive.microsoft.com/vision/v1.0/ocr";

    HttpResponseMessage response;
```

```
// Construct a well-formed JSON key/value pair that
// represents the image URL
JObject imageUrl = new JObject(
                    new JProperty("url",
                    "http://community.visual-basic.it/images/community_
                    visual-basic_it/Alessandro/184/o_OcrSample.jpg")));

// You pass the JSON object above as the request body
using (var content =
    new StringContent(imageUrl.ToString(), Encoding.UTF8, "application/
    json"))
{
    // Add headers
    content.Headers.ContentType = new MediaTypeHeaderValue("application/
    json");

    // Call the endpoint
    response = await client.PostAsync(uri, content);

    // If successful,
    if (response.StatusCode == HttpStatusCode.OK)
    {
        // Read the resulting HTTP content as a string
        string jsonResponse = await response.Content.
        ReadAsStringAsync();

        // Generate fully indented JSON markup from the original
        response
        var parsedJson = JObject.Parse(jsonResponse);
        Console.WriteLine(parsedJson.ToString());
    }

}

Console.ReadLine();
}
```

The response you get from the Computer Vision's OCR service for the specified image looks like the following JSON:

```
{
  "language": "en",
  "textAngle": -2.0000000000000338,
  "orientation": "Up",
  "regions": [
    {
      "boundingBox": "92,165,467,136",
      "lines": [
```

```json
{
  "boundingBox": "97,165,451,57",
  "words": [
    {
      "boundingBox": "97,165,8,42",
      "text": "I"
    },
    {
      "boundingBox": "126,167,106,44",
      "text": "CAN"
    },
    {
      "boundingBox": "255,171,293,51",
      "text": "RECOGNIZE"
    }
  ]
},
{
  "boundingBox": "92,243,467,58",
  "words": [
    {
      "boundingBox": "92,243,159,46",
      "text": "WHAT"
    },
    {
      "boundingBox": "265,249,108,45",
      "text": "YOU"
    },
    {
      "boundingBox": "393,253,166,48",
      "text": "WRITE"
    }
  ]
}
        ]
      }
    ]
  }
]
}
```

The JSON response consists of the following core elements:

- regions: An array of objects where each represents a region of detected text

- lines: An array of objects where each represents a line of text in a region

- words: An array of objects where each represents a single word in a line

When you want to parse detected text with OCR, you need to remember this more complex hierarchy. Of course, you can still use the JObject class to parse the content of the JSON response as you saw previously.

Retrieving Handwritten Text

The Computer Vision API also offers an interesting service that allows you to retrieve handwritten text from images. Its behavior is similar to the OCR service, but you call the following endpoint: https://[location].api.cognitive.microsoft.com/vision/v1.0/recognizeText[?handwriting]. What you need to do here is supply the handwriting=true query string parameter to enable handwritten text recognition. If you don't specify this parameter, the service will search for printed text via OCR.

Working with Domain-Specific Models

With domain-specific models, Computer Vision algorithms can perform specialized analysis over specific categories of images. At this writing, the Computer Vision API offers two domain-specific models out of the box: celebrity recognition and landmark recognition. The list of domain-specific models will certainly increase in the future, and you'll have an option to create your own.

Imagine you want to detect celebrities in a picture. First, you need to retrieve the list of domain-specific models and get a reference to the celebrity recognition. This is accomplished with an HTTP GET request against the https://[location].api.cognitive.microsoft.com/vision/v1.0/models endpoint, like in the following code:

```
async static Task ListModelsAsync()
{
    var client = new HttpClient();

    // Add the subscription key to the header
    client.DefaultRequestHeaders.Add("Ocp-Apim-Subscription-Key", "YOUR-KEY-
    GOES-HERE");

    // Define the API endpoint
    string uri = "https://westus.api.cognitive.microsoft.com/vision/v1.0/models";

    HttpResponseMessage response;

    // Call the endpoint
    response = await client.GetAsync(uri);

    // If successful,
    if (response.StatusCode == HttpStatusCode.OK)
    {
        // Read the resulting HTTP content as a string
        string jsonResponse = await response.Content.ReadAsStringAsync();
```

```
    // Generate fully indented JSON markup from the original response
    var parsedJson = JObject.Parse(jsonResponse);
    Console.WriteLine(parsedJson.ToString());
}

Console.ReadLine();
}
```

The previous call will return the following JSON (which might vary in the future):

```
{
  "models": [
    {
      "name": "celebrities",
      "categories": [
        "people_"
      ]
    },
    {
      "name": "landmarks",
      "categories": [
        "outdoor_",
        "building_"
      ]
    }
  ],
  "requestId": "d7a81873-fdf9-4e48-8247-26b1ec0725b4"
}
```

As you can see, there is an array called models. For each item in the array, you will want to check the value of the name property, such as celebrities or landmarks. This must be passed to the endpoint that performs the actual recognition over an image. The URL of the endpoint for recognizing domain-specific content is as follows: https://[location].api.cognitive.microsoft.com/vision/v1.0/models/{model}/analyze. Here you will need to replace [location] with the domain name of the closest Azure region and {model} with either celebrities or landmarks. For copyright reasons, I will neither show figures with celebrities nor point to existing image URLs about celebrities, but you can use the following code to retrieve the result of celebrity recognition over an image:

```
async static Task RecognizeCelebrityAsync()
{
    var client = new HttpClient();

    // Add the subscription key to the header
    client.DefaultRequestHeaders.Add("Ocp-Apim-Subscription-Key", "YOUR-KEY-
    GOES-HERE");
```

```csharp
    // Define the API endpoint
    string uri = "https://westus.api.cognitive.microsoft.com/vision/v1.0/
models/celebrities/analyze";

    HttpResponseMessage response;

    // Construct a well-formed JSON key/value pair that
    // represents the image URL
    JObject imageUrl = new JObject(
                        new JProperty("url",
                        "IMAGE-URL-GOES-HERE"));

    // You pass the JSON object above as the request body
    using (var content =
        new StringContent(imageUrl.ToString(), Encoding.UTF8, "application/
        json"))
    {
        // Add headers
        content.Headers.ContentType = new MediaTypeHeaderValue("application/
        json");

        // Call the endpoint
        response = await client.PostAsync(uri, content);

        // If successful,
        if (response.StatusCode == HttpStatusCode.OK)
        {
            // Read the resulting HTTP content as a string
            string jsonResponse = await response.Content.
            ReadAsStringAsync();

            // Generate fully indented JSON markup from the original
            response
            var parsedJson = JObject.Parse(jsonResponse);
            Console.WriteLine(parsedJson.ToString());
        }

    }

    Console.ReadLine();
}
```

The JSON response you get looks like the following:

```json
{
  "requestId": "ab594260-2d70-4919-b997-425cddd9758d",
  "metadata": {
    "width": 960,
```

41

```
    "height": 540,
    "format": "Jpeg"
  },
  "result": {
    "celebrities": [
      {
        "name": "Celebrity name",
        "faceRectangle": {
          "left": 346,
          "top": 74,
          "width": 75,
          "height": 75
        },
        "confidence": 0.9925701
      }
    ]
  }
}
```

The JSON response contains the image information in the metadata item and an array called celebrities. This contains a list of all the celebrity names that have been detected in an image, and for each celebrity you can see the coordinates for the face. As for the other endpoints, you can use the JObject class to parse the JSON result into .NET objects. Landmarks recognition works in the same way, but instead of the celebrities array you have one called landmarks.

Summary

The Computer Vision API provides powerful and sophisticated algorithms that allow you to describe and analyze images with natural language descriptions. To query the service, you send HTTP POST and GET requests to the various endpoints. In C#, and more generally in .NET, this can be done with the System.Net.Http.HttpClient class, which is portable across platforms and therefore can be used on all the .NET platforms and with all the Microsoft IDEs, such as Visual Studio 2017, Visual Studio for Mac, and Visual Studio Code.

After creating and configuring a console application on Windows, macOS, and Ubuntu, you walked through the Computer Vision API capabilities, by first learning how to describe an image with a natural language, machine-generated description. You then saw how to retrieve more complex results with image analysis. The discussion then moved to show how to generate thumbnails and tags, with easy API calls. Moving on, you saw how the OCR engine is powerful enough to recognize printed text and handwritten text within images. Finally, you got started with domain-specific models, learning how to get a list of available models and then how to perform celebrity recognition. In all the code examples, you used the JObject class to both construct and parse JSON objects.

So far you have seen how to invoke the Computer Vision API, and you learned how to send requests and parse the JSON response in the form of strings. In the next chapter, you will start consuming the Computer Vision API with mobile apps using Xamarin. Forms and a different approach based on the Computer Vision Client Library.

CHAPTER 4

■ ■ ■

Computer Vision on Mobile Apps with Xamarin

Artificial intelligence provides tremendous benefits to users if it is available everywhere. With mobile devices and mobile apps, this is certainly possible. For this reason, for you, as a developer, understanding how you can consume Cognitive Services in your mobile apps is extremely important.

From the point of view of C# development, Xamarin is certainly the technology you will want to consider for mobile app development. With Xamarin, you can build native apps for Android, iOS, macOS, and tvOS in C#. Additionally, with Xamarin.Forms, you can write native apps for Android, iOS, and Windows 10 with a single, shared C# codebase that allows you to create cross-platform solutions. This chapter introduces you to the wonderful world of Computer Vision on mobile devices with Xamarin.Forms, and I'm sure you will immediately perceive the incredible opportunities that AI opens to mobile developers.

■ **Note**   In this chapter, you will use emulators to run the iOS, Android, and Windows 10 versions of the sample project. However, for real-world mobile development, I strongly recommend you work on physical devices.

Creating a Xamarin.Forms Solution

One of the goals of this chapter is to explain how you can consume the Computer Vision API (and, more generally, Microsoft Cognitive Services) on multiple mobile platforms. In terms of mobile app development, Xamarin.Forms is certainly the most appropriate choice since it allows you to create apps for iOS, Android, and Windows 10 from a single C# codebase. More specifically, you will see how to create an app whose user interface is made of three tabs, allowing for describing images, recognizing text, and recognizing celebrities.

To build a Xamarin.Forms solution, you need Visual Studio 2017 on Windows or Visual Studio for Mac on macOS. The free Community edition of both IDEs fully support Xamarin.Forms development. I will now describe the steps to create and configure a new sample Xamarin.Forms solution on both systems.

© Alessandro Del Sole 2018
A. Del Sole, *Microsoft Computer Vision APIs Distilled,*
https://doi.org/10.1007/978-1-4842-3342-9_4

■ **Note** Because the goal of this chapter is not introducing Xamarin.Forms and rather is describing how to invoke the Computer Vision API from a Xamarin.Forms solution, a minimum knowledge of Xamarin.Forms is strongly recommended to complete this chapter. If you do not have experience with it, you can start for free with my *Xamarin.Forms Succinctly* e-book, available at `http://bit.ly/2gegT9l`. I will assume you know how to create a page and how to use the Extensible Application Markup Language (XAML) to design a basic user interface.

Configuring Visual Studio 2017 for Xamarin

■ **Note** If you already installed the Xamarin development tools along with Visual Studio 2017, you can skip this section. You do not need any additional configurations on Visual Studio for Mac, which already includes all the required tools, assuming you selected the Xamarin components at installation time.

Before you can get started with Xamarin development in Visual Studio 2017, you must install the proper tools. To accomplish this, you first need to start the Visual Studio Installer tool, and then you have to select the "Mobile development with .NET" workload, as shown in Figure 4-1.

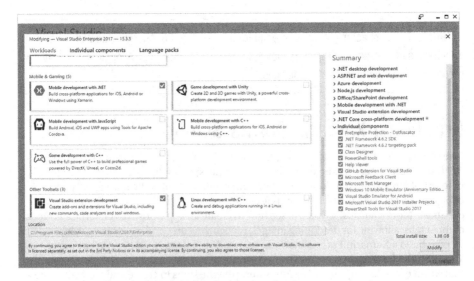

Figure 4-1. *Installing the Xamarin development tools*

At this point, click the "Individual components" tab, locate the Emulators group, and make sure that at least the following components are selected:

- Google Android Emulator

- Intel Hardware Accelerated Execution Manager

- Windows 10 Mobile Emulator (select the highest Windows version possible)

When ready, click Modify. The Visual Studio Installer will take a few minutes to install the selected components. When the installation completes, you can close the Visual Studio Installer and start Visual Studio 2017.

Introducing the Computer Vision Client Library

In the previous chapter, you saw how to use the System.Net.HttpClient class to perform HTTP requests against the Computer Vision API service, and then you used the Newtonsoft.Json namespace to parse the JSON response. This approach is the most versatile because it can be easily reused across platforms, but it requires you to implement your own .NET objects to represent the analysis result over images, and it requires you to manually specify headers, content types, endpoints, and query string parameters when you create an instance of HttpClient and when you invoke its methods (typically PostAsync and GetAsync).

Microsoft has also developed a client portable library that encapsulates HTTP requests into specific methods and that exposes classes that you can use to easily deserialize the analysis result into .NET strongly typed objects. This library is called Microsoft.ProjectOxford.Vision.dll and is available as a NuGet package.

▓ **Note**　Project Oxford was the project name for Microsoft Cognitive Services before it was released.

In solutions where you work with portable libraries, this library can dramatically simplify the way you interact with the Computer Vision API. For this reason, it perfectly fits into a Xamarin.Forms solution, and, in this chapter, you will learn how to use this library instead of the other approach so that you have full knowledge of all the ways to query the Computer Vision service. Table 4-1 lists the most important types and members provided by the library.

Table 4-1. *Most Important Types and Members in the Microsoft.ProjectOxford.Vision Library*

Name	Type	Description
VisionServiceClient	Class	Provides managed access to the Computer Vision API and allows you to specify a subscription key
AnalyzeImageAsync	Method	Allows you to analyze and describe an image
RecognizeTextAsync	Method	Performs OCR over images containing text
AnalyzeImageInDomainAsync	Method	Allows you to analyze images based on domain-specific models such as celebrities and landmarks
AnalysisResult	Class	Represents the response for the analysis result on an image
AnalysisInDomainResult	Class	Represents the response for the image analysis based on domain-specific models
VisualFeature	Enum	Represents information that must be returned from querying the Computer Vision service

These types and members will be discussed in more detail shortly, when creating the sample app's pages.

Mentioning this library before creating the Xamarin.Forms solution was necessary so that you know what it is when installing all the necessary NuGet packages.

Creating a Xamarin.Forms Solution in Visual Studio 2017

In Visual Studio 2017, select File ➤ New ➤ Project. In the New Project dialog, locate the Cross-Platform node and then select the Cross-Platform App (Xamarin) project template, as shown in Figure 4-2. Enter **ComputerVisionDemo** as the project name and then click OK.

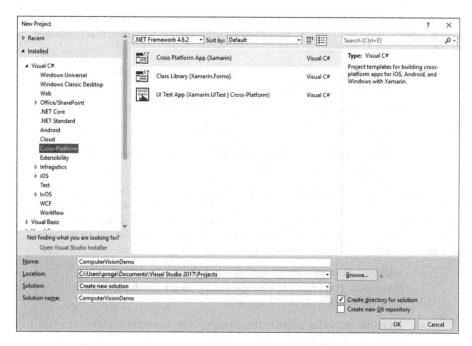

Figure 4-2. *Creating a Xamarin.Forms solution*

In the next dialog, Visual Studio will ask you to specify the UI technology and the code-sharing strategy. Select Xamarin.Forms and Portable Class Library (PCL), respectively (see Figure 4-3).

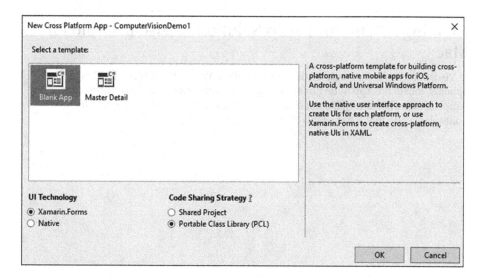

Figure 4-3. *Configuring a Xamarin.Forms solution*

Click OK when ready. When prompted, select the highest version of Windows 10 you want to target. After a few seconds, Visual Studio will generate a solution that is made of the following:

- A Portable Class Library (PCL) project that will contain all the shared code across platforms

- A Xamarin.Android project that targets Android devices

- A Xamarin.iOS project that targets iOS devices

- A Universal Windows Platform (UWP) project that targets Windows 10 devices and machines

The PCL project is the place where you write all the code that can be shared across platforms, which includes the user interface and all the code that is not platform-specific. You will now need a few NuGet packages, which you install by right-clicking the solution name in Solution Explorer and then selecting Manage NuGet Packages. When the NuGet user interface appears, you will need to install the following packages:

- Microsoft.ProjectOxford.Vision, the client library described previously. This library has a dependency on the Newtonsoft.Json package, which will also be installed.

- Xam.Plugin.Media, a library that makes it easy to access media files with cross-platform code.

- Xam.Plugin.Connectivity, a library that allows you to check for Internet connection availability with cross-platform code.

The solution is now set up. A guide about Visual Studio for Mac will be now provided, and then you will start writing code.

Creating a Xamarin.Forms Solution in Visual Studio for Mac

In Visual Studio for Mac, select File > New Solution. When the New Project dialog appears, locate the App node under Multiplatform and select the Blank Forms App template (see Figure 4-4). Do not choose the Forms App template, as it contains boilerplate code that is not useful for this example.

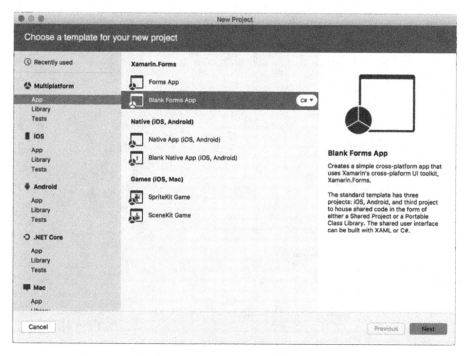

Figure 4-4. Creating a Xamarin.Forms solution on the Mac

When you click Next, you will be asked to enter a project name (see Figure 4-5). Enter **ComputerVisionDemo** and make sure that Use Portable Class Library and "Use XAML for user interface files" are both selected.

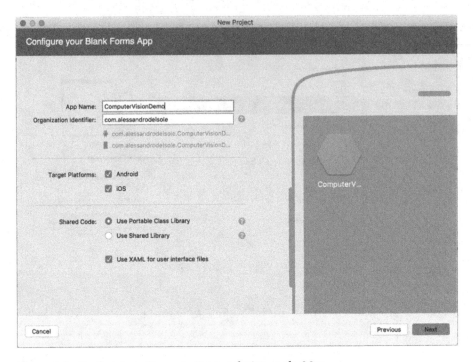

Figure 4-5. *Configuring a Xamarin.Forms solution on the Mac*

Remember that Xamarin.Forms solutions created with Visual Studio for Mac do not support the Universal Windows Platform project type. Click Next and wait for the solution to be created. Now you need to install some NuGet packages. Differently from Visual Studio 2017 on Windows, in Visual Studio for Mac you cannot install packages directly at the solution level. This means you need to install the same NuGet package into each individual project. To install one or more NuGet packages into a project, you need to right-click the project name in the Solution pad and then select Add ➤ Add Nuget Packages. When the Add Packages dialog appears, you can search for and select multiple packages to be installed into the same project. The packages you need are the following:

- Microsoft.ProjectOxford.Vision, the client library described previously. This package is required only in the PCL project of your solution and has a dependency on the Newtonsoft.Json package, which will also be installed.

- Xam.Plugin.Media, a library that makes it easy to access media files with cross-platform code. This package must be installed into all the projects in the solution.

- Xam.Plugin.Connectivity, a library that allows you to check for Internet connection availability with cross-platform code. This package must be installed into all the projects in the solution.

Once you have completed installing NuGet packages, you are ready to consume the Computer Vision API from your Xamarin solution.

Instantiating the Service Client

The Computer Vision Client Library provides a class called VisionServiceClient, from the Microsoft.ProjectOxford.Vision namespace, that allows you to communicate with the Computer Vision API service in a totally .NET-oriented fashion. You therefore need an instance of this class, and a good place to create one is in the App class and the App.xaml. cs file.

This way, you will have a single instance that will serve for multiple requests in different app pages. The following code demonstrates how to declare and create a shared instance of the VisionServiceClient class:

```
using Microsoft.ProjectOxford.Vision;
using Xamarin.Forms;

namespace ComputerVisionDemo
{
    public partial class App : Application
    {
        internal static VisionServiceClient visionClient;
        public App()
        {
            InitializeComponent();

            visionClient = new VisionServiceClient("YOUR-KEY-GOES-HERE",
                "https://YourAzureRegion.api.cognitive.microsoft.com/vision/
                v1.0");
            MainPage = new ComputerVisionDemo.MainPage();
        }
    }
}
```

Notice how the constructor takes two string parameters: the first parameter represents your subscription key, and the second parameter is the root service URL, where you will need to replace the part about the Azure region with one of the URLs summarized in Chapter 2.

Implementing Image Analysis

The first feature you're going to implement is to analyze and describe images, taking advantage of the Computer Vision Client Library. This will be offered through a specific page, which will be later embedded into the app's main page.

First, add a new XAML content page to the PCL project. In Visual Studio 2017, you accomplish this by right-clicking the project name and then selecting Add ➤ New Item. In Visual Studio for Mac, you accomplish this by right-clicking the project name and then selecting Add ➤ New File. In both cases, select the ContentPage XAML item template and call the new page ImageAnalysisPage.xaml. When you add the page, Visual Studio also generates a C# code-behind file, in this case ImageAnalysisPage.xaml.cs. This is the place where you will write the code that uploads an image to the Computer Vision service for analysis and gets a response. This can be done by invoking the AnalyzeImageAsync method of the VisionServiceClient class, encapsulating the logic as follows:

```
private async Task<AnalysisResult> AnalyzePictureAsync(Stream inputFile)
{
    // Use the connectivity plugin to detect
    // if a network connection is available
    // Remember a using Plugin.Connectivity; directive
    if (!CrossConnectivity.Current.IsConnected)
    {
        await DisplayAlert("Network error",
            "Please check your network connection and retry.", "OK");
        return null;
    }

    VisualFeature[] visualFeatures = new VisualFeature[] { VisualFeature.
    Adult,
        VisualFeature.Categories, VisualFeature.Color, VisualFeature.
        Description,
        VisualFeature.Faces, VisualFeature.ImageType, VisualFeature.Tags };

    AnalysisResult analysisResult =
        await App.visionClient.AnalyzeImageAsync(inputFile,
        visualFeatures);

    return analysisResult;
}
```

This code first checks for Internet connection availability by leveraging the CrossConnectivity class from the Xam.Plugin.Connectivity library. Then it creates an array of VisualFeature objects, each representing a piece of information you want to retrieve from the image. VisualFeature is actually an enumeration, and the array combines multiple members. This is how VisualFeature is implemented behind the scenes:

```
namespace Microsoft.ProjectOxford.Vision
{
    public enum VisualFeature
    {
        ImageType = 0,
        Color = 1,
        Faces = 2,
        Adult = 3,
```

```
        Categories = 4,
        Tags = 5,
        Description = 6
    }
}
```

The AnalyzeImageAsync method receives two arguments: the input file, which is a stream, and the array of VisualFeature objects. The result is wrapped into an object of type AnalysisResult and is defined as follows:

```
namespace Microsoft.ProjectOxford.Vision.Contract
{
    public class AnalysisResult
    {
        public AnalysisResult();

        public Guid RequestId { get; set; }
        public Metadata Metadata { get; set; }
        public ImageType ImageType { get; set; }
        public Color Color { get; set; }
        public Adult Adult { get; set; }
        public Category[] Categories { get; set; }
        public Face[] Faces { get; set; }
        public Tag[] Tags { get; set; }
        public Description Description { get; set; }
    }
}
```

Each of this class's properties is a specialized type. It is a good idea to look at how they are defined; you need to know where the information you need is actually stored because you might want to perform data-binding from the user interface to these objects. In the current sample app, you'll take into consideration the Color, Adult, Category, Face, Tags, and Description types. By the way, the sample app will use only a few properties from these types, so Table 4-2 summarizes the properties that will be used. If you want to see the full type definition, you can simply right-click the type name in the code editor and then select Go To Definition.

Table 4-2. *Most Common Properties for Image Analysis*

Property	Class	Description	Type
AccentColor	Color	Returns the dominant color in a picture	string
IsAdultContent	Adult	Returns true if an image contains explicit content	bool
IsRacyContent	Adult	Returns true if an image contains racy content	bool
Captions	Description	An array of Caption type made of a Text string property and a Confidence double property that represents the human language description of an image	Caption[]

You then need some code that allows the user either to pick an existing image from the device or to take a new picture from the built-in camera. To accomplish this, you can take advantage of the Xam.Plugin.Media library and write the following code that is related to two buttons that will be declared soon in the UI (also notice that Indicator1 is an ActivityIndicator control that will be placed in the user interface in a few moments):

```
private async void TakePictureButton_Clicked(object sender, EventArgs e)
{
    await CrossMedia.Current.Initialize();

    if (!CrossMedia.Current.IsCameraAvailable || !CrossMedia.Current.
    IsTakePhotoSupported)
    {
        await DisplayAlert("No Camera", "No camera available.", "OK");
        return;
    }

    var file = await CrossMedia.Current.TakePhotoAsync(new
    StoreCameraMediaOptions
    {
        SaveToAlbum = true,
        Name = "test.jpg"
    });

    if (file == null)
        return;

    this.Indicator1.IsVisible = true;
    this.Indicator1.IsRunning = true;
```

```
    Image1.Source = ImageSource.FromStream(() => file.GetStream());
    this.BindingContext = await AnalyzePictureAsync(file.GetStream());

    this.Indicator1.IsRunning = false;
    this.Indicator1.IsVisible = false;
}

private async void UploadPictureButton_Clicked(object sender, EventArgs e)
{
    if (!CrossMedia.Current.IsPickPhotoSupported)
    {
        await DisplayAlert("No upload", "Picking a photo is not supported.", "OK");
        return;
    }

    var file = await CrossMedia.Current.PickPhotoAsync();
    if (file == null)
        return;

    this.Indicator1.IsVisible = true;
    this.Indicator1.IsRunning = true;
    Image1.Source = ImageSource.FromStream(() => file.GetStream());

    try
    {
        this.BindingContext = await AnalyzePictureAsync(file.GetStream());
    }
    catch (Exception ex)
    {
        await DisplayAlert("Error", ex.Message, "OK");
        return;
    }
    finally
    {
        this.Indicator1.IsRunning = false;
        this.Indicator1.IsVisible = false;
    }
}
```

■ **Note** In the previous code, the result of the AnalyzePictureAsync method is assigned to the BindingContext property directly only for demonstration purposes. In real-world code, you will want to create a proper view model that will also serve as the data source for the user interface.

Here are some points of interest in the previous code:

- The CrossMedia class from the Xam.Plugin.Media library allows you to pick an existing image or take one from the camera with the PickPhotoAsync and TakePhotoAsync methods, respectively.

- TakePhotoAsync allows you to specify a file name and whether the file should be saved to the Camera Roll.

- The selected picture is assigned to the Source property of an Image control, called Image1, and must be passed as an open stream to the AnalyzePictureAsync method defined previously.

- The instance of the AnalysisResult class returned from AnalyzePictureAsync is assigned to the page's BindingContext property as the data source for the user interface. This allows for data-binding controls to properties in the AnalysisResult instance, as you will see shortly in the XAML code.

Now let's see how to allow users to select images and how to display the analysis results in the user interface for the current page.

Designing the User Interface

The XAML code of the user interface of the current page is simple. A root StackLayout contains an Image control, where the selected image will be displayed, an ActivityIndicator control to display a progress indicator, and a ScrollView, whose content is a set of Label controls bound to properties of the AnalysisResult object, as well as a ListView control that will display, via data binding, a list of detected tags. The XAML code looks like the following:

```
<?xml version="1.0" encoding="utf-8" ?>
<ContentPage xmlns="http://xamarin.com/schemas/2014/forms" Title="Analysis"
             xmlns:x="http://schemas.microsoft.com/winfx/2009/xaml"
             x:Class="ComputerVisionDemo.ImageAnalysisPage">
  <ContentPage.Content>
    <StackLayout Orientation="Vertical">
      <Button x:Name="TakePictureButton" Clicked="TakePictureButton_
      Clicked"
     Text="Take from camera"/>
      <Button x:Name="UploadPictureButton"
      Clicked="UploadPictureButton_Clicked"
     Text="Pick a photo"/>
      <ActivityIndicator x:Name="Indicator1" IsVisible="False"
      IsRunning="False" />
      <Image x:Name="Image1" HeightRequest="240" WidthRequest="320" />

      <ScrollView Padding="10">
        <StackLayout>
```

```xml
<StackLayout Orientation="Horizontal">
    <Label Text="Adult content: "/>
    <Label Text="{Binding Adult.IsAdultContent}"/>
</StackLayout>
<StackLayout Orientation="Horizontal">
    <Label Text="Racy content: "/>
    <Label Text="{Binding Adult.IsRacyContent}"/>
</StackLayout>
<StackLayout Orientation="Horizontal">
    <Label Text="Description: "/>
    <Label Text="{Binding Description.Captions[0].Text}"/>
</StackLayout>
<StackLayout Orientation="Horizontal">
    <Label Text="Accent color: "/>
    <Label Text="{Binding Color.AccentColor}"/>
</StackLayout>
<StackLayout Orientation="Horizontal">
    <Label Text="Tags: "/>
    <ListView ItemsSource="{Binding Tags}">
        <ListView.ItemTemplate>
            <DataTemplate>
                <ViewCell>
                    <Label Text="{Binding Name}"/>
                </ViewCell>
            </DataTemplate>
        </ListView.ItemTemplate>
    </ListView>
</StackLayout>
</StackLayout>
</ScrollView>
</StackLayout>
</ContentPage.Content>
</ContentPage>
```

Points of interest in the previous XAML code are represented by the `Binding` expressions, each pointing to properties of the `AnalysisResult` class and their child properties. It's interesting to mention that the first element in the `Description.Captions` array (with index zero) contains the natural language description for the image. You will now see how to implement optical character recognition.

Implementing Optical Character Recognition

The Computer Vision Client Library also simplifies optical character recognition over images, and the approach is similar to image analysis, in that you invoke a method called `RecognizeTextAsync` from the `VisionServiceClient` class, passing the image you want to analyze and getting an object of type `OcrResults` as a response. Having that said, add a new XAML content page to the PCL project, called `OcrRecognitionPage.xaml`.

In the C# code-behind file, you can write the following method to implement OCR recognition on an image file passed as a stream:

```
private async Task<OcrResults> AnalyzePictureAsync(Stream inputFile)
{
    if (!CrossConnectivity.Current.IsConnected)
    {
        await DisplayAlert("Network error", "Please check your network
        connection and retry.", "OK");
        return null;
    }

    OcrResults ocrResult = await App.visionClient.
RecognizeTextAsync(inputFile);
    return ocrResult;
}
```

As you did previously, you can use the CrossConnectivity class to detect Internet connection availability. The OcrResults class is more complex than AnalysisResult. Among other features, it exposes a Regions property of type Region[ ]. Each Region in the array represents a region of text the service was able to recognize and exposes a Lines property of type Line[ ]. Each line in the array represents a single line in the region and exposes a Words property of type Word[ ]. Each Word in the array represents a word in the line, and its Text property contains the actual word. Because of this more complex structure, one possible way of retrieving the recognized text is to iterate regions, then lines, and then words. For example, you can create a number of StackLayout containers with a number of labels representing the detected text as follows:

```
private void PopulateUIWithRegions(OcrResults ocrResult)
{
    // Iterate the regions
    foreach (var region in ocrResult.Regions)
    {
        // Iterate lines per region
        foreach (var line in region.Lines)
        {
            // For each line, add a panel
            // to present words horizontally
            var lineStack = new StackLayout
            { Orientation = StackOrientation.Horizontal };

            // Iterate words per line and add the word
            // to the StackLayout
            foreach (var word in line.Words)
            {
                var textLabel = new Label { Text = word.Text };
                lineStack.Children.Add(textLabel);
            }
```

```
        // Add the StackLayout to the UI
        this.DetectedText.Children.Add(lineStack);
    }
  }
}
```

DetectedText is a root StackLayout container in the UI, and the PopulateUIWithRegions method will be invoked after retrieving the OCR result with AnalyzePictureAsync. Now exactly as you did for image analysis, you can implement two Button.Clicked event handlers, one for picking an image from the device's disk and one for taking a picture from the camera:

```
private async void UploadPictureButton_Clicked(object sender, EventArgs e)
{
    if (!CrossMedia.Current.IsPickPhotoSupported)
    {
        await DisplayAlert("No upload", "Picking a photo is not supported.", "OK");
        return;
    }

    var file = await CrossMedia.Current.PickPhotoAsync();
    if (file == null)
        return;

    this.Indicator1.IsVisible = true;
    this.Indicator1.IsRunning = true;
    Image1.Source = ImageSource.FromStream(() => file.GetStream());

    var ocrResult = await AnalyzePictureAsync(file.GetStream());
    this.BindingContext = ocrResult;

    PopulateUIWithRegions(ocrResult);

    this.Indicator1.IsRunning = false;
    this.Indicator1.IsVisible = false;
}

private async void TakePictureButton_Clicked(object sender, EventArgs e)
{
    await CrossMedia.Current.Initialize();

    if (!CrossMedia.Current.IsCameraAvailable || !CrossMedia.Current.
    IsTakePhotoSupported)
    {
        await DisplayAlert("No Camera", "No camera available.", "OK");
        return;
    }
```

```
var file = await CrossMedia.Current.TakePhotoAsync(new StoreCameraMediaOptions
{
    SaveToAlbum = true,
    Name = "test.jpg"
});

if (file == null)
    return;

this.Indicator1.IsVisible = true;
this.Indicator1.IsRunning = true;

Image1.Source = ImageSource.FromStream(() => file.GetStream());

var ocrResult = await AnalyzePictureAsync(file.GetStream());
this.BindingContext = null;
this.BindingContext = ocrResult;

PopulateUIWithRegions(ocrResult);

this.Indicator1.IsRunning = false;
this.Indicator1.IsVisible = false;
}
```

Notice how the result of the OCR is assigned to the BindingContext property of the page. The reason is that the user interface will data-bind a label to the Language property of the OcrResults class, which contains the language for the recognized text. Then notice how an invocation to PopulateUIWithRegions will populate the UI with all the individual lines of text.

Designing the User Interface

The user interface for this page is even simpler, since it contains the Image control to display the selected image, two buttons, an ActivityIndicator to display the progress indicator, a data-bound Label to display the language, and a scrollable StackLayout that will be populated at runtime with the PopulateUIWithRegions method. The XAML markup looks like the following:

```
<?xml version="1.0" encoding="utf-8" ?>
<ContentPage xmlns="http://xamarin.com/schemas/2014/forms" Title="OCR"
             xmlns:x="http://schemas.microsoft.com/winfx/2009/xaml"
             x:Class="ComputerVisionDemo.OcrRecognitionPage">

  <StackLayout Orientation="Vertical">
    <Button x:Name="TakePictureButton" Clicked="TakePictureButton_Clicked"
        Text="Take from camera"/>
```

```xml
<Button x:Name="UploadPictureButton" Clicked="UploadPictureButton_Clicked"
    Text="Pick a photo"/>
<ActivityIndicator x:Name="Indicator1" IsVisible="False" IsRunning="False" />
<Image x:Name="Image1" HeightRequest="240" />

<StackLayout Orientation="Horizontal">
  <Label Text="Language: "/>
  <Label Text="{Binding Language}"/>
</StackLayout>

<ScrollView>
  <StackLayout x:Name="DetectedText"/>
</ScrollView>

  </StackLayout>
</ContentPage>
```

You're almost done. The next step is to implement celebrity recognition, and then you will be able to see the results of your work in action.

Implementing Celebrity Recognition

Celebrity recognition is part of the domain-specific models available in the Computer Vision API. At this writing, this service supports celebrity and landmark recognition as domain-specific models. Regarding domain-specific models, the Computer Vision Client Library provides the VisionServiceClient.AnalyzeImageInDomainAsync method, which returns an object of type AnalysisInDomainResult.

To understand how it works, add a new page to the PCL project called CelebrityRecognitionPage.xaml. In the C# code-behind, add the following method:

```csharp
private async Task<AnalysisInDomainResult> AnalyzePictureAsync(Stream
inputFile)
{
    if (!CrossConnectivity.Current.IsConnected)
    {
        await DisplayAlert("Network error", "Please check your network
connection and retry.", "OK");
        return null;
    }

    AnalysisInDomainResult analysisResult =
        await App.visionClient.AnalyzeImageInDomainAsync(inputFile, await
        GetDomainModel());

    return analysisResult;
}
```

As you can see, the AnalyzeImageInDomainAsync method requires the input file as a parameter but also an object of type Model that represents the domain-specific model against which the image must be analyzed. In this case, this object is returned by a method called GetDomainModel, whose code is as follows:

```
private async Task<Model> GetDomainModel()
{
    ModelResult modelResult = await App.visionClient.ListModelsAsync();
    // At this writing, only celebrity recognition
    // is available. It is the first model in the list
    return modelResult.Models.First();
}
```

The ListModelsAsync method returns the list of available domain-specific models. The first model in the list is about celebrities, but you can select a different one. Parsing the AnalysisInDomainResult object returned at the end of the analysis is more complex because its Result property is of type object, and therefore you must do some manual parsing. The result is actually JSON markup that contains an element called celebrities, which contains an array of celebrity names, each identified by the name property. Put succinctly, you could use the Newtonsoft.Json.Linq.JObject class to parse JSON content into string contents as follows:

```
private string ParseCelebrityName(object analysisResult)
{
    JObject parsedJSONresult = JObject.Parse(analysisResult.ToString());

    var celebrities = from celebrity in parsedJSONresult["celebrities"]
                      select (string)celebrity["name"];

    return celebrities.FirstOrDefault();
}
```

Notice that, for the sake of keeping the UI simple, the previous code is returning only one celebrity name. You can change the code to remove FirstOrDefault and return an IEnumerable<string> if you want to handle multiple celebrity names. As you did previously, you can now handle two Button.Clicked events as follows:

```
private async void TakePictureButton_Clicked(object sender, EventArgs e)
{
    await CrossMedia.Current.Initialize();

    if (!CrossMedia.Current.IsCameraAvailable || !CrossMedia.Current.
    IsTakePhotoSupported)
    {
        await DisplayAlert("No Camera", "No camera available.", "OK");
        return;
    }
```

```
    var file = await CrossMedia.Current.TakePhotoAsync(new
    StoreCameraMediaOptions
    {
        SaveToAlbum = true,
        Name = "test.jpg"
    });

    if (file == null)
        return;

    this.Indicator1.IsVisible = true;
    this.Indicator1.IsRunning = true;

    Image1.Source = ImageSource.FromStream(() => file.GetStream());

    var analysisResult = await AnalyzePictureAsync(file.GetStream());
    this.CelebrityName.Text = ParseCelebrityName(analysisResult.Result);

    this.Indicator1.IsRunning = false;
    this.Indicator1.IsVisible = false;
}

private async void UploadPictureButton_Clicked(object sender, EventArgs e)
{
    if (!CrossMedia.Current.IsPickPhotoSupported)
    {
        await DisplayAlert("No upload", "Picking a photo is not supported.",
        "OK");
        return;
    }

    var file = await CrossMedia.Current.PickPhotoAsync();
    if (file == null)
        return;

    this.Indicator1.IsVisible = true;
    this.Indicator1.IsRunning = true;
    Image1.Source = ImageSource.FromStream(() => file.GetStream());

    AnalysisInDomainResult analysisResult = await AnalyzePictureAsync(file.
    GetStream());
    this.CelebrityName.Text = ParseCelebrityName(analysisResult.Result);

    this.Indicator1.IsRunning = false;
    this.Indicator1.IsVisible = false;
}
```

In this particular case, there is no data binding. There is only a label called CelebrityName whose Text property is assigned with the result of ParseCelebrityName. If you change the code to handle multiple celebrity names, you will obviously need multiple labels or a ListView control.

Designing the User Interface

The XAML code for the user interface of this page is really simple. At the core, you need an Image control to display the selected image and a Label to display the celebrity name:

```
<?xml version="1.0" encoding="utf-8" ?>
<ContentPage xmlns="http://xamarin.com/schemas/2014/forms" Title="Celebrity"
             xmlns:x="http://schemas.microsoft.com/winfx/2009/xaml"
             x:Class="ComputerVisionDemo.CelebrityRecognitionPage">
  <StackLayout Orientation="Vertical">
    <Button x:Name="TakePictureButton" Clicked="TakePictureButton_Clicked"
        Text="Take from camera"/>
    <Button x:Name="UploadPictureButton" Clicked="UploadPictureButton_
Clicked"
        Text="Pick a photo"/>
    <ActivityIndicator x:Name="Indicator1" IsVisible="False"
IsRunning="False" />
    <Image x:Name="Image1" HeightRequest="240" />

    <Label x:Name="CelebrityName"/>
  </StackLayout>
</ContentPage>
```

It's now time to put all the pages together and see how the app works.

Putting It All Together

The final step in the sample Xamarin.Forms solution is to create a tabbed page that includes the content pages created previously. To accomplish this, you can change the content of the MainPage.xaml page from a ContentPage object to a TabbedPage object, whose XAML markup looks like this:

```
<?xml version="1.0" encoding="utf-8" ?>
<TabbedPage xmlns="http://xamarin.com/schemas/2014/forms"
            xmlns:x="http://schemas.microsoft.com/winfx/2009/xaml"
            xmlns:local="clr-namespace:ComputerVisionDemo"
            x:Class="ComputerVisionDemo.MainPage">
```

```
<TabbedPage.Children>
    <local:ImageAnalysisPage />
    <local:OcrRecognitionPage />
    <local:CelebrityRecognitionPage />
</TabbedPage.Children>
</TabbedPage>
```

Notice how you add ContentPage objects to the TabbedPage.Children property and Xamarin.Forms will resolve the appropriate layout based on the system the app is running on. In the C# code-behind, you need to change the inheritance for the MainPage object, from ContentPage to TabbedPage, as follows:

```
public partial class MainPage : TabbedPage
{

    public MainPage()
    {
        InitializeComponent();
    }
}
```

Now you are ready to test your sample app, but there is a last step you must do, which is enabling permissions to access the camera and the picture library on the desired platforms. For the UWP project, you do not need to change the application manifest since all the necessary permissions are already set. For the Android project, you need to select the following permissions in the application manifest: CAMERA, INTERNET, READ_EXTERNAL_STORAGE. For the iOS project, in the Info.plist file you need to include the NSCameraUsageDescription and NSPhotoLibraryUsageDescription properties with a string description to support privacy restrictions in iOS 10 and higher. At this point, select your target platform and start debugging using the toolbar or keyboard shortcuts available on your system. Figure 4-6 shows an example of image description on the Windows tablet simulator, whereas Figure 4-7 shows an example of OCR based on the iOS simulator. For copyright reasons, I will not show the result for celebrity recognition, but you can try yourself.

Figure 4-6. *The sample app running on a Windows 10 tablet*

Figure 4-7. *The sample app performing OCR on the iPhone*

As you can see, depending on the image quality, your app will be able to perform sophisticated analysis over images. Implementing computer vision in your mobile apps opens up infinite scenarios and will help you build the next generation of intelligent apps.

Summary

Artificial intelligence is extremely useful on mobile apps, because users can have apps empowered by intelligent algorithms in their pockets, wherever they go. Based on this, this chapter introduced how to consume the Computer Vision API on mobile apps developed with Xamarin.Forms.

You saw how to create a Xamarin.Forms solution on both Visual Studio 2017 and Visual Studio for Mac and how to configure the solution with the proper NuGet packages. You then got an overview of a different approach to querying the Computer Vision API, based on the Computer Vision Client Library, represented by the Microsoft.ProjectOxford. Vision package, which exposes types and members that allow for executing operations and retrieving results in a totally .NET-oriented fashion. The discussion then moved to the practical implementation of the analysis operations, including describing images, performing OCR, and recognizing celebrities, also leveraging useful Xamarin plug-ins. The biggest benefit of using the Client Library is that you do not need to perform complex JSON parsing, as you instead get strongly typed .NET objects to represent the response returned by the service. Together with the implementation, you saw how to design basic user interfaces and how to test the sample application in the emulators. The next chapter gives you instead an overview of another interesting opportunity, which is consuming the Computer Vision API from ASP.NET web applications.

CHAPTER 5

■ ■ ■

Computer Vision in Web Apps with ASP.NET MVC Core

Bringing artificial intelligence to mobile apps, as you saw in Chapter 4, is extremely interesting for many reasons, not only from the point of view of the opportunities you have as a developer but also because you empower users to do more with a device they have in their pockets.

However, like in other development scenarios, you should never forget about people working on PCs in office workstations or home offices. For example, imagine how artificial intelligence in the healthcare industry could help doctors to identify patients' symptoms or emotions and generate appropriate reports. This could be done with mobile devices, but probably doctors work on PCs at their desks, and the environment is potentially a private intranet, with custom web applications that can connect to a webcam.

Because Cognitive Services can be consumed by any application on any platform, they can also be consumed within an ASP.NET web application. By saying ASP.NET, I mean ASP.NET MVC on the .NET Framework, ASP.NET MVC Core on .NET Core, and Web API services on both the .NET Framework and .NET Core. In this chapter, I will demonstrate how to consume the Computer Vision API in an ASP.NET MVC Core application on Windows, macOS, and Ubuntu. Keep in mind that the same concepts apply to ASP.NET on the .NET Framework. This chapter's focus is not on explaining ASP. NET MVC Core, so you can take a look at the official documentation (`http://docs.microsoft.com/en-us/aspnet/core`) for further details.

■ **Note** This chapter assumes you already have configured your development environment with Visual Studio 2017, Visual Studio for Mac, or Visual Studio Code, depending on your operating system. Take a look at Chapter 3 for more information on configuring the development environment.

© Alessandro Del Sole 2018
A. Del Sole, *Microsoft Computer Vision APIs Distilled,*
https://doi.org/10.1007/978-1-4842-3342-9_5

Creating an ASP.NET MVC Core Application

ASP.NET MVC Core is a lightweight, open source, cross-platform framework that allows you to build web applications that run on Windows, macOS, and Linux (and its more popular distributions), using C# and the Model-View-Controller pattern on the .NET Core runtime. If you have experience with ASP.NET MVC on the .NET Framework, you will be familiar with its .NET Core counterpart. The goal of this chapter is to explain how you can create a web application that uploads an image file to the Computer Vision API, displaying the analysis result on a web page.

I will first explain how to generate a new ASP.NET MVC Core application on the three operating systems introduced in Chapter 3; then I will explain the C# code you can use to send the image for analysis and parse and display the response.

Creating the Web Application with Visual Studio 2017

In Visual Studio 2017, select File ➤ New ➤ Project. In the New Project dialog, locate the .NET Core category. Then select the ASP.NET Core Web Application template, as shown in Figure 5-1. Call the new project **WebComputerVision** and then click OK.

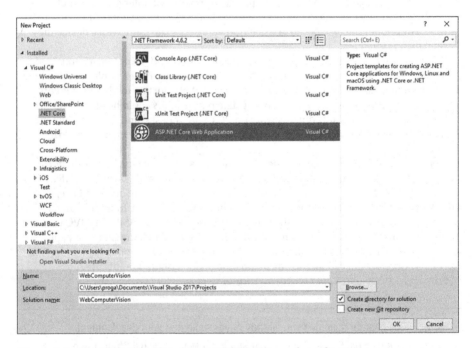

Figure 5-1. *The project template for an ASP.NET Core web application*

In the next dialog, you will be asked to specify what kind of application you want to create. Select the Web Application (Model-View-Controller) template (see Figure 5-2) and then click OK.

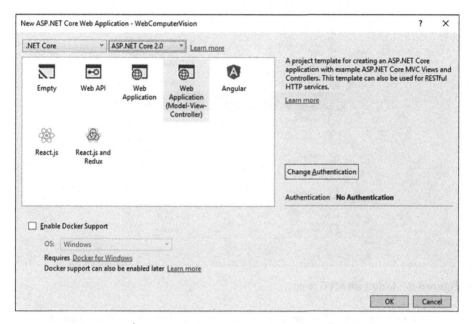

Figure 5-2. *Creating an MVC project*

■ **Note**   Notice how you can configure the authentication mechanism and how you can enable support for packaging your application into a Docker container. Regarding authentication, you can select individual authentication (username and password), Office 365 authentication, Windows authentication for intranets, and anonymous authentication (the default). This is a nice option because Visual Studio will generate the necessary infrastructure to support authentication.

Once the project has been created, the next step is to add a new web page that will be used to display the controls required to upload the image and to display the analysis results. For the sake of simplicity, this page can be added to the Views\Home folder. So, right-click this folder in Solution Explorer and then select Add ➤ New Item. In the Add New Item dialog, select the MVC View Page item, as demonstrated in Figure 5-3.

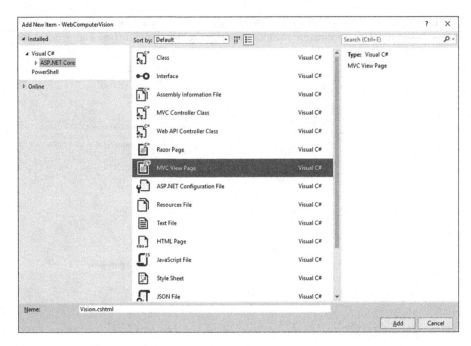

Figure 5-3. *Adding an MVC page*

Make sure the name of the page is `Vision.cshtml` and then click Add. To avoid extra complexity, in this case there is no need to add a dedicated controller class; the `HomeController` class will be used. This will be demonstrated later. For now, let's move on to configuring the project by installing the Newtonsoft.Json NuGet package. Exactly as you did in Chapter 3, right-click the project name in Solution Explorer and then select Manage NuGet Packages. When the NuGet window appears, search for the Newtonsoft. Json package and click Install. This package will be used to deserialize and parse the JSON response returned by the Computer Vision service.

Creating the Web Application with Visual Studio for Mac

In Visual Studio for Mac, select File ➤ New Solution. In the New Project dialog, locate the ASP.NET Core Web App project template under .NET Core ➤ App, as demonstrated in Figure 5-4. When ready, click Next.

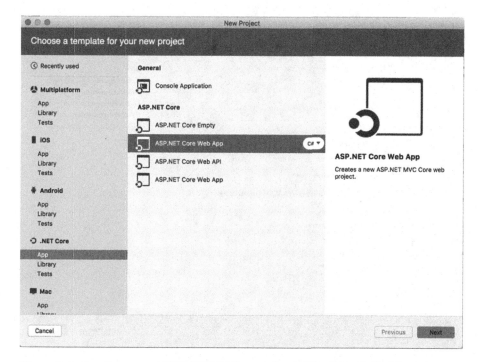

Figure 5-4. Creating a new ASP.NET MVC Core project in Visual Studio for Mac

---

■ **Note**   If you see two ASP.NET Core Web App templates, select the first one in the list, as shown in Figure 5-4. The second project template generates a web project based on Razor views, but I'm not discussing Razor in this book.

If you have multiple versions of .NET Core installed, you will be asked to select the runtime version. Select .NET Core 2.0 and click Next. In the end, you will be asked to supply the project name, as shown in Figure 5-5, so enter **WebComputerVision** and click Create.

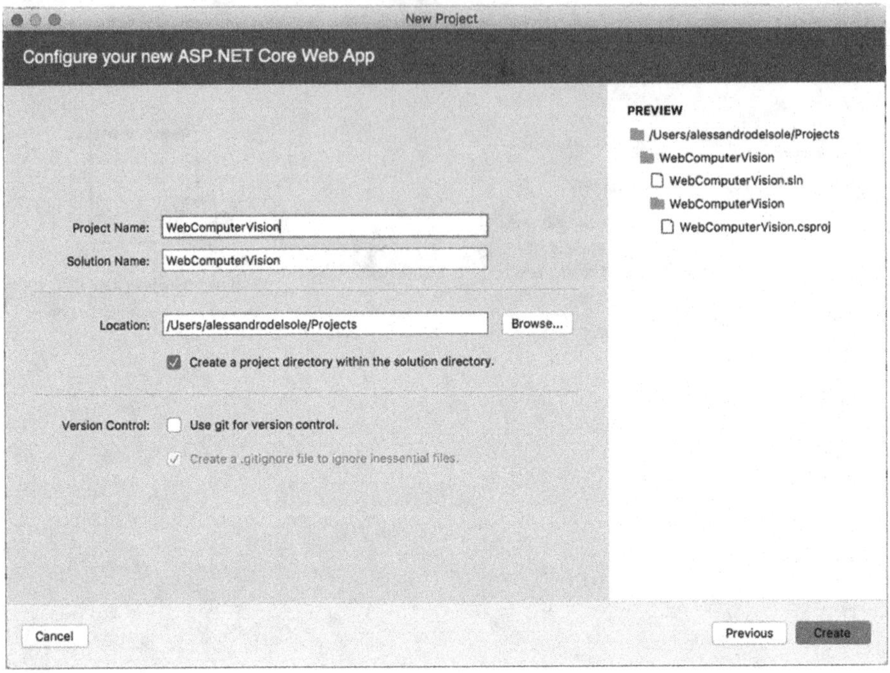

Figure 5-5. *Providing a project name*

For Visual Studio 2017 on Windows, you need to add a new web page that will display the user controls required to upload an image and display the analysis results. To accomplish this, right-click the Views\Home folder in the Solution pad and then select Add ➤ New File. In the New File dialog, select the MVC View Page template, and enter **Vision** as the page name, as represented in Figure 5-6; then click New.

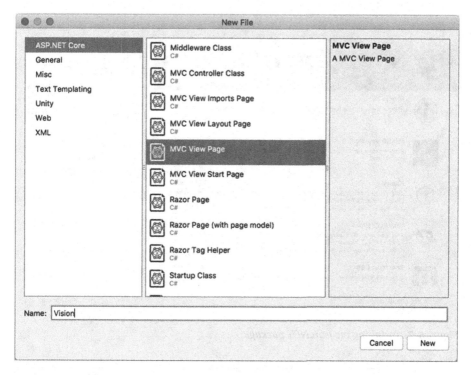

Figure 5-6. *Adding a new MVC page*

The last step is to install from NuGet a library that you can use to parse and deserialize JSON contents. Exactly as you did in Chapter 3, in the Solution pad right-click the project name and then select Add ➤ Add NuGet Packages. When the NuGet dialog appears, search for the Json.NET package and then click Add Package (see Figure 5-7).

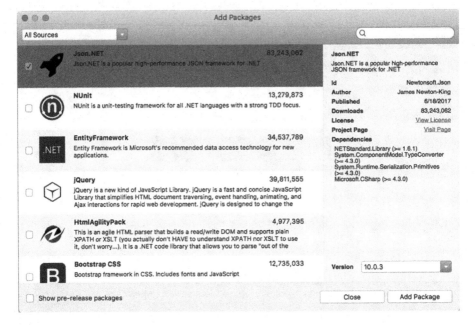

Figure 5-7. *Installing the Json.NET package*

■ **Note** Remember that Json.NET and Newtonsoft.Json are the same thing, but Visual Studio 2017 shows the package ID (Newtonsoft.Json) and Visual Studio for Mac shows the package name.

Now the project is configured, so you can move on to creating an ASP.NET MVC Core application on Ubuntu with Visual Studio Code.

Creating the Web Application with Visual Studio Code

As you learned in Chapter 3, you can create .NET applications on Linux and its more popular distributions using C# and Visual Studio Code. However, the latter has no built-in options to create a new project, so you have to use the `dotnet` command-line tool. This will be demonstrated on Ubuntu. Follow these steps:

1. With the Files program, open the Home folder and create a new subfolder called `WebComputerVision`.

-2. Enter the new folder, right-click, and select Open in Terminal.

3. When an instance of the Terminal is started, type the following command line, which will scaffold a new, empty ASP.NET MVC project with the same structure you saw in Visual Studio 2017 and Visual Studio for Mac:

   ```
   > dotnet new mvc
   ```

4. Open the new project in Visual Studio Code with the following command line:

   ```
   > code.
   ```

When Visual Studio Code starts and the new project is opened, accept the prompt to generate the required assets; then in the Explorer bar, locate the Views\Home folder. Right-click, select New File, and rename the new file to Vision.cshtml. This file represents a new web page that will be used to display controls required to upload an image file to the Computer Vision API and the analysis result.

The next step is adding the Newtonsoft.Json NuGet package to the project. As you might remember from Chapter 3, to accomplish this, you need to select the .csproj project file in the Explorer bar, and then you add a PackageReference element as follows:

```
<ItemGroup>
  <PackageReference Include="Microsoft.AspNetCore.All" Version="2.0.0" />
  <PackageReference Include="Newtonsoft.Json" Version="10.0.3" />
</ItemGroup>
```

Now click File ➤ Save All so that Visual Studio Code will be able to restore all packages and to refresh references. At this point, you have an ASP.NET MVC Core project configured on all the three major platforms, and you can start writing code in the editor of your choice.

Implementing the Controller

In an MVC application, URLs are mapped to controllers, which are C# classes that process incoming requests, handle user input, and execute application logic. When you create a new ASP.NET MVC Core application with .NET Core, the project contains one controller class, called HomeController and defined in the HomeController.cs file. This class exposes methods (technically *actions*) that are invoked when the user clicks hyperlinks in the user interface and that therefore are mapped to a page's content via HTML markup that you will see in the next section.

For the current example, it is necessary to implement, inside a controller, a method (the action) that will be mapped to the Vision.cshtml page added previously to the project. Though common practice in real-world applications, in this particular case and for the sake of simplicity, it's not necessary to create a separate controller, so the HomeController class can be extended for our purposes. Currently, the HomeController controller contains four action methods: Index, mapped to the Index.cshtml page;

About, mapped to the About.cshtml page; Contact, mapped to the Contact.cshtml page; and Error, mapped to a generic error page. A new action called Vision will be added to the controller. The code for the action is simple and looks like the following:

```
public IActionResult Vision()
{
    ViewData["Message"] = "Picture analysis";

    return View();
}
```

This method returns to the same-named page, assigning the ViewData dynamic object with a string that will be displayed in the page. You then need to implement the real action that will be responsible for sending the HTTP request to the Computer Vision service, including the image file. In the case of Computer Vision, Face, and Emotion APIs, the image file must be read as a Stream object, which must be serialized into a base-64 string and then wrapped into a byte array. So, before you implement the action, you need some code that reads the image file and serializes it into a byte array. This is accomplished with the following code:

```
private string BytesToSrcString(byte[] bytes) => "data:image/jpg;base64," +
Convert.ToBase64String(bytes);

// IFormFile represents a file that can be sent
// with HTTP requests
private string FileToImgSrcString(IFormFile file)
{
    byte[] fileBytes;
    using (var stream = file.OpenReadStream())
    {

        using (var memoryStream = new MemoryStream())
        {
            stream.CopyTo(memoryStream);
            fileBytes = memoryStream.ToArray();
        }
    }
    return BytesToSrcString(fileBytes);
}
```

Now that you have a way of reading the image file as a stream and of serializing it into a byte array, you can implement the Vision action as follows (see comments in the code):

```
private const string apiKey = "YOUR-KEY-GOES-HERE";

[HttpPost]
[ValidateAntiForgeryToken]
public async Task<IActionResult> Vision(IFormFile file)
```

```
{
    //put the original file in the view data
    ViewData["originalImage"] = FileToImgSrcString(file);
    string result = null;

    using (var httpClient = new HttpClient())
    {
        // Request parameters (Replace [location] with the domain name of
        your Azure region)
        string baseUri = "https://[location].api.cognitive.microsoft.com/
        vision/v1.0/describe";

        //set up HttpClient
        httpClient.BaseAddress = new Uri(baseUri);
        httpClient.DefaultRequestHeaders.Add("Ocp-Apim-Subscription-Key",
        apiKey);

        //set up data object
        HttpContent content = new StreamContent(file.OpenReadStream());
        content.Headers.ContentType = new MediaTypeWithQualityHeaderValue("a
        pplication/octet-stream");

        //make request
        var response = await httpClient.PostAsync(baseUri, content);

        // get the string for the JSON response
        string jsonResponse = await response.Content.ReadAsStringAsync();

        // You can replace the following code with customized or
        // more precise JSON deserialization
        var jresult = JObject.Parse(jsonResponse);
        result = jresult["description"]["captions"][0]["text"].ToString();
    }

    ViewData["result"] = result;
    return View();
}
```

The code here is invoking the endpoint that allows for describing an image, but
of course you can use a different endpoint. Also, notice how the code here is using
deserialization techniques with the JObject class you used in Chapter 3. Of course,
depending on the endpoint you invoke and on the response you expect, you can
implement different deserialization techniques. In this particular case, the first natural
language description returned by the service is retrieved and returned to the caller page,
which is the Vision.cshtml page you added previously and that will be designed in the
next section.

Designing the View

The user interface of the Vision.cshtml page that will be used to select and upload an image file and to display the analysis results is simple. A Form object contains Label controls used to display some text, an Input control allows a user to select a file, and another Input control starts the upload operation; in addition, an Img control is used to display the selected image, and another Label is used to display the result of the invocation to the Computer Vision service. The complete markup for the page looks like the following:

```
@{
    ViewData["Title"] = "Vision";
}
<h2>@ViewData["Title"].</h2>
<h3>@ViewData["Message"]</h3>

<div class="row">
    <div class="col-md-12">
        <form asp-action="Vision" enctype="multipart/form-data">
            <div class="form-horizontal">
                <div class="form-group">
                    <label for="file">Image</label>
                    <input type="file" name="file" id="file" class="form-
                    control">
                    <p class="help-block">Images must be up to 4 megabytes
                    and greater than 50x50</p>
                </div>
                <div class="form-group">
                    <input type="submit" value="Upload" class="btn btn-
                    primary" />
                </div>
            </div>
        </form>
    </div>
</div>

<div class="row">
    <div class="col-md-12">
        <h4>Original Image</h4>
        <img src="@ViewData["originalImage"]" />
    </div>
</div>

<div class="row">
    <div class="col-md-12">
        <h4>Result</h4>
```

```
        <label>@ViewData["result"]</label>
    </div>
</div>
```

Notice how the page can receive data from the related action by using the ViewData object (in ASP.NET MVC, the @ symbol allows you to include C# code in the markup). Once you have designed the page, you have to add it to the list of pages available for the application. To accomplish this, open the _Layout.cshtml file located under Views\ Shared, and add the following line highlighted in bold in the code block that groups the available pages:

```
<div class="navbar-collapse collapse">
    <ul class="nav navbar-nav">
        <li><a asp-area="" asp-controller="Home" asp-action="Index">Home
        </a></li>
        <li><a asp-area="" asp-controller="Home" asp-action="About">About
        </a></li>
        <li><a asp-area="" asp-controller="Home" asp-action="Contact">
        Contact</a></li>
        <li><a asp-area="" asp-controller="Home" asp-action="Vision">
        Vision</a></li>
    </ul>
</div>
```

Notice how asp-controller specifies the associated controller class (the Controller literal is omitted) and how asp-action allows you to specify the action in the controller to be associated to the page. Now that the page is ready, you can test the application.

Testing the Application

Regardless of the development environment and of the operating system you are using, you can start the application with the debugging tools you already know. For example, you can press F5 in Visual Studio 2017, press Command+Enter in Visual Studio for Mac, or click the "Start debugging" button in the Debug pane in Visual Studio Code.

It is important to know that, for local debugging, ASP.NET MVC Core uses a web server called Kestrel (http://docs.microsoft.com/en-us/aspnet/core/fundamentals/ servers/kestrel). Kestrel is an open source, cross-platform development server that can be used to host web applications at debugging time, and both Visual Studio for Mac and Visual Studio Code automatically use Kestrel when you start debugging. Visual Studio 2017 on Windows is not limited to using Kestrel, and it also allows you to select IIS Express as the host. For the sake of consistency across platforms, for this example make sure you select Kestrel as the development server in Visual Studio 2017. To accomplish this, expand the menu of the Start button and select your project name, as shown in Figure 5-8.

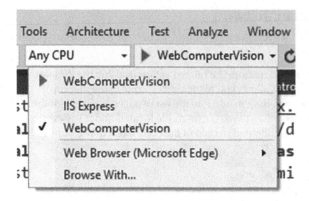

Figure 5-8. *In Visual Studio 2017, selecting the project name enables the Kestrel debugger.*

When the application starts in debug mode, the .NET Core execution environment also starts the Kestrel service in a console application. By default, Kestrel works with the `http://localhost:5000` address. However, Visual Studio 2017 allows you to change the port in the project properties. When the application starts in your browser, it will look like Figure 5-9.

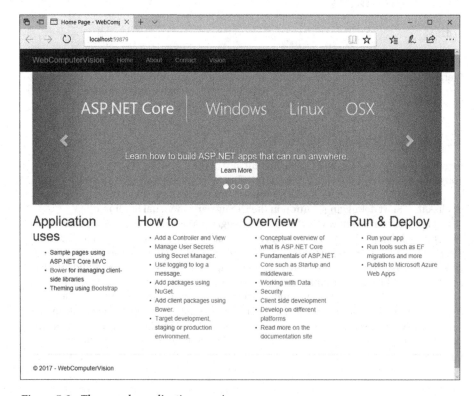

Figure 5-9. *The sample application running*

As you can see, a hyperlink called Vision is available in the upper-right corner. If you click this hyperlink, the Vision page will appear and will look like Figure 5-10.

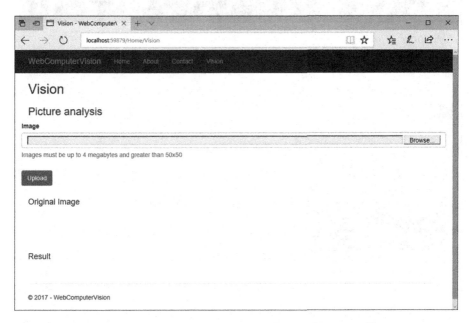

Figure 5-10. *The user interface designed to select and upload an image file*

Here you can click the Browse button, select an image file, and, when ready, click the Upload button. If the selected image is valid, the Computer Vision API will return a description that will be displayed in the page, together with the selected image, as shown in Figure 5-11.

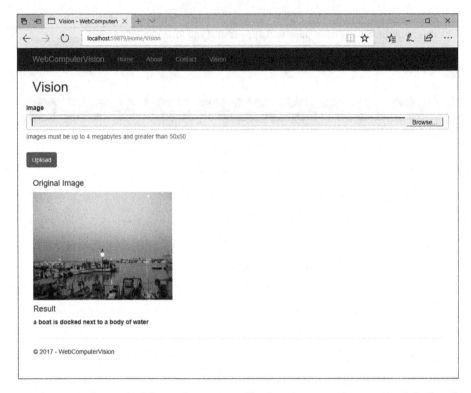

Figure 5-11. *The result of the analysis returned by the Computer Vision API and displayed in the web page*

Let's now try to see the behavior of the application by using OCR instead of the image description. First, in the HomeController.cs file, change the baseUri variable with the following declaration:

```
string baseUri = "https://[location].api.cognitive.microsoft.com/vision/
v1.0/ocr";
```

where [location] must be replaced with the domain name of your Azure region. Then, replace the following line:

```
result = jresult["description"]["captions"][0]["text"].ToString();
```

With the following loop that parses regions, lines, and words (see Chapter 3 for a recap about OCR responses):

```
foreach(var region in jresult["regions"])
{
    foreach(var line in region["lines"])
    {
        foreach(var word in line["words"])
        {
            result = result + " " + word["text"].ToString();
        }
    }
}
```

If you now restart the application and select an image that contains text, you will see how the page correctly shows the result of the OCR recognition, if the operation succeeds. Figure 5-12 shows an example.

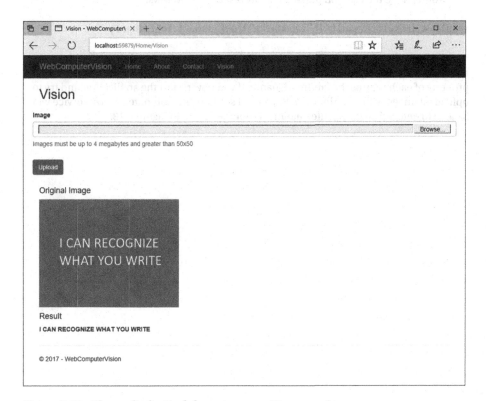

Figure 5-12. *The result of optical character recognition on an image*

The last example is instead based on a domain-specific model, in particular on landmarks recognition. In the C# code, replace the value of the baseUri variable with the following:

```
string baseUri = "https://[location].api.cognitive.microsoft.com/vision/
v1.0/models/landmarks/analyze";
```

As usual, [location] must be replaced with the name of your Azure region.

■ **Note**   In the previous chapters, you saw how to perform an HTTP GET request to retrieve the list of domain-specific models that you can use with the previous endpoint. Obviously, if you know in advance the exact name of the domain model, like in the current example, you can avoid the GET request.

Now change the way you parse the JSON response as follows:

```
result = jresult["result"]["landmarks"][0]["name"].ToString();
```

Among other things, the JSON response contains an array called result, with as many landmarks arrays as landmarks that have been detected in a picture; the name property of each returns the landmark name. If you now restart the application and try to upload an image with a landmark in it, you will see how the Computer Vision service will be able to detect the correct information, as demonstrated in Figure 5-13.

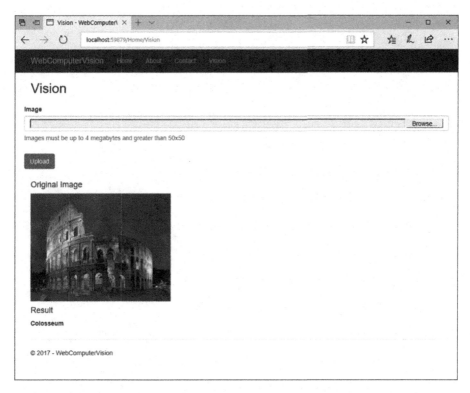

Figure 5-13. *Landmarks recognition*

The Computer Vision API can really enhance web applications for both the enterprise and the world of consumers, with powerful image analysis algorithms that help you to create next-generation applications. In addition, with .NET Core, all this power is also available for the macOS and Linux systems.

Summary

In this chapter, you saw how to leverage the power of the Computer Vision API in a web application built with ASP.NET MVC Core. At the beginning, you saw how to create the same sample project on three different systems with Visual Studio 2017, Visual Studio for Mac, and Visual Studio Code.

Then you saw how to implement an action inside a controller to read an image file from disk and send it to the Computer Vision service for describing its content. Next, you saw how to design a web page that contains controls to select and upload the image and that display the analysis result. Finally, you saw how to test the application locally, demonstrating how powerful web applications that leverage artificial intelligence can be.

Index

© Alessandro Del Sole 2018
A. Del Sole, *Microsoft Computer Vision APIs Distilled*,
https://doi.org/10.1007/978-1-4842-3342-9

Get the eBook for only $5!

Why limit yourself?

With most of our titles available in both PDF and ePUB format, you can access your content wherever and however you wish—on your PC, phone, tablet, or reader.

Since you've purchased this print book, we are happy to offer you the eBook for just $5.

To learn more, go to http://www.apress.com/companion or contact support@apress.com.

Apress®

Printed in the United States
By Bookmasters